The Concise
MASTERY

ALSO BY ROBERT GREENE

The 50th Law (with 50 Cent)

The 33 Strategies of War
(A Joost Elfers Production)

The Art of Seduction
(A Joost Elfers Production)

The 48 Laws of Power
(A Joost Elfers Production)

The Concise

MASTERY

ROBERT GREENE

P
PROFILE BOOKS

This concise edition published in Great Britain in 2014 by
PROFILE BOOKS LTD
3A Exmouth House
Pine Street
London EC1R 0JH
www.profilebooks.com

Derived from *Mastery*, which was first published in Great Britain in 2012 by
Profile Books and in the United States of America in 2012 by Viking,
a division of Penguin Putnam Inc.

21

Printed and bound in India by
Manipal Technologies Limited, Manipal

A CIP catalogue record for this book is available from the British Library.

ISBN 978 1 84668 156 1
eISBN 978 1 84765 342 0

To Anna

CONTENTS

II.
SUBMIT TO REALITY: THE IDEAL APPRENTICESHIP

IV.
SEE PEOPLE AS THEY ARE: SOCIAL INTELLIGENCE

VI.
FUSE THE INTUITIVE WITH
THE RATIONAL: MASTERY   175

INTRODUCTION

THE ULTIMATE POWER

> *Everyone holds his fortune in his own hands, like a sculptor the raw material he will fashion into a figure. But it's the same with that type of artistic activity as with all others: We are merely born with the capability to do it. The skill to mold the material into what we want must be learned and attentively cultivated.*

—Johann Wolfgang von Goethe

There exists a form of power and intelligence that represents the high point of human potential. It is the source of the greatest achievements and discoveries in history. It is an intelligence that is not taught in our schools nor analyzed by professors, but almost all of us, at some point, have had glimpses of it in our own experience. It often comes to us in a period of tension—facing a deadline, the urgent need to solve a problem, a crisis of sorts.

1

Or it can come as the result of constant work on a project. In any event, pressed by circumstances, we feel unusually energized and focused. Our minds become completely absorbed in the task before us. This intense concentration sparks all kinds of ideas—they come to us as we fall asleep, out of nowhere, as if springing from our unconscious. At these times, other people seem less resistant to our influence; perhaps we are more attentive to them, or we appear to have a special power that inspires their respect. We might normally experience life in a passive mode, constantly reacting to this or that incident, but for these days or weeks we feel like we can determine events and make things happen.

We could express this power in the following way: Most of the time we live in an interior world of dreams, desires, and obsessive thoughts. But in this period of exceptional creativity, we are impelled by the need to get something done that has a practical effect. We force ourselves to step outside our inner chamber of habitual thoughts and connect to the world. At these moments, suddenly exposed to new details and ideas, we become more inspired and creative.

Once the deadline has passed or the crisis is over, this feeling of power and heightened creativity generally fades away. We return to our distracted state and the sense of control is gone.

The problem we face is that this form of power and intelligence is either ignored as a subject of study or is surrounded by all kinds of myths and misconceptions, all of which only add to the mystery. We imagine that creativity and brilliance just appear out of nowhere, the fruit of natural talent, or perhaps of a good mood, or an alignment of the stars. It would be an immense help to clear up the mystery—to name this feeling of power, and to understand how it can be manufactured and maintained.

Let us call this sensation *mastery*—the feeling that we have a greater command of reality, other people, and ourselves. Although it might be something we experience for only a short while, for others—Masters of their field—it becomes their way of life, their way of seeing the world. And at the root of this power is a simple process that leads to mastery—one that is accessible to all of us.

The process can be illustrated in the following manner: Let us say we are learning the piano, or entering a new job where we must acquire certain skills. In the beginning, we are outsiders. Our initial impressions of the piano or the work environment are based on prejudgments, and often contain an element of fear. When we first study the piano, the keyboard looks rather intimidating—we don't understand the relationships between the keys, the chords, the pedals, and everything else that goes into creating music. In a new job situation, we are ignorant of the power relationships between people, the psychology of our boss, the rules and procedures that are considered critical for success. We are confused—the knowledge we need in both cases is over our heads.

Although we might enter these situations with excitement about what we can learn or do with our new skills, we quickly realize how much hard work there is ahead of us. The great danger is that we give in to feelings of boredom, impatience, fear, and confusion. We stop observing and learning. The process comes to a halt.

If, on the other hand, we manage these emotions and allow time to take its course, something remarkable begins to take shape. As we continue to observe and follow the lead of others, we gain clarity, learning the rules and seeing how things work and fit together. If we keep practicing, we gain fluency; basic skills are mastered, allowing us to take on newer and more exciting challenges.

At a certain point, we move from student to practitioner. We try out our own ideas, gaining valuable feedback in the process. We use our expanding knowledge in ways that are increasingly creative. Instead of just learning how others do things, we bring our own style and individuality into play.

As years go by and we remain faithful to this process, yet another leap takes place—to mastery. The keyboard is no longer something outside of us; it is internalized and becomes part of our nervous system, our fingertips. In our career, we now have a feel for the group dynamic, the current state of business. We can apply this feel to social situations, seeing deeper into other people and anticipating their reactions. We can make decisions that are rapid and highly creative. Ideas come to us. We have learned the rules so well that we can now be the ones to break or rewrite them.

In the process leading to this ultimate form of

power, we can identify three distinct phases or levels. The first is the *Apprenticeship;* the second is the *Creative-Active;* the third, *Mastery.* In the first phase, we stand on the outside of our field, learning as much as we can of the basic elements and rules. In the second phase, through much practice and immersion, we see into the inside of the machinery, how things connect with one another, and thus gain a more comprehensive understanding of the subject. With this comes a new power— the ability to experiment and creatively play with the elements involved. In the third phase, our degree of knowledge, experience, and focus is so deep that we can now see the whole picture with complete clarity.

We can call this power intuition, but intuition is nothing more than a sudden and immediate seizing of what is real, without the need for words or formulas.

Intuitive powers at the mastery level are a mix of the instinctive and the rational, the conscious and the unconscious, the human and the animal. It is our way of making sudden and powerful connections to the environment, to feeling or thinking inside things. As children we had some of this intuitive power and spontaneity, but it is generally drummed out of us by all of the information that overloads our minds over time. Masters return to this childlike state, their works displaying degrees of spontaneity and access to the unconscious, but at a much higher level than the child.

If we move through the process to this endpoint, we activate the intuitive power latent in every human brain, one that we may have briefly experienced when we worked so deeply on a single problem or project. When we reach mastery, this intuition is a power at our command, the fruit of working through the lengthier process.

Think of mastery in this way: Throughout history, men and women have felt trapped by the limitations of their consciousness, by their lack of contact with reality and the power to affect the world around them. They have sought all kinds of shortcuts to this expanded consciousness and sense of control, in the form of magic rituals, trances, incantations, and drugs.

This hunger for the magical shortcut has survived to our day in the form of simple formulas for success, ancient secrets finally revealed in which a mere change of attitude will attract the right energy. All of this searching is centered on something that doesn't exist—the effortless path to practical power, the quick and easy solution, the El Dorado of the mind.

At the same time that so many people lose themselves in these endless fantasies, they ignore the one real power that they actually possess. And unlike magic or simplistic formulas, we can see the material effects of this power in history—the great discoveries and inventions, the magnificent buildings and works of art, the technological prowess we possess, all works of the masterful mind. This power brings to those who possess it the kind of connection to reality and the ability to alter the world that the mystics and magicians of the past could only dream of.

Over the centuries, people have placed a wall around such mastery. They have called it genius and have thought of it as inaccessible. They have seen it as the product of privilege, inborn talent, or just the right alignment of the stars. They have made it seem as if it were as elusive as magic. But that wall is imaginary. This is the real secret: the brain that we possess is the work of six million years of development, and more than anything else, this evolution of the brain was designed to lead us to mastery, the latent power within us all.

KEYS TO MASTERY

If all of us are born with an essentially similar brain, with more or less the same configuration and potential for mastery, why is it then that in history only a limited number of people seem to truly excel and realize this potential power? Certainly, in a practical sense, this is the most important question for us to answer.

The common explanations for a Mozart or a Leonardo da Vinci revolve around natural talent and brilliance. But thousands upon thousands of children display exceptional skill and talent in some field, yet relatively few of them ever amount to anything, whereas those who are less brilliant in their youth can often attain much more. Natural talent or a high IQ cannot explain future achievement.

What we find instead in the stories of all great masters is essentially the following pattern: a youthful passion or predilection, a chance encounter that allows them to discover how to apply it, an apprenticeship in which they come alive with energy and focus. They excel by their ability to practice harder and move faster through the process, all of this stemming from the intensity of their desire to learn and from the deep connection they feel to their field of study. And at the core of this intensity of effort is, in fact, a quality that is genetic and inborn—not talent or brilliance, which is something that must be developed, but rather a deep and powerful inclination toward a particular subject.

This inclination is a reflection of a person's uniqueness. This uniqueness is not something merely poetic or philosophical—it is a scientific fact that genetically, every one of us is unique; our exact genetic makeup has never happened before and will never be repeated. This uniqueness is revealed to us through the preferences we innately feel for particular activities or subjects of study. Such inclinations can be toward music or mathematics, certain sports or games, solving puzzle-like problems, tinkering and building, or playing with words.

With those who stand out by their later mastery, they experience this inclination more deeply and clearly than others. They experience it as an inner calling. It tends to dominate their thoughts and dreams. They find their way, by accident or sheer effort, to a career path in which this inclination can flourish. This intense connection and desire allows them to withstand the pain of the process—the self-doubts, the tedious hours of practice and study, the inevitable setbacks, the endless barbs from the envious. They develop a resiliency and confidence that others lack.

In our culture we tend to equate thinking and intellectual powers with success and achievement. In many ways, however, it is an emotional quality that separates those who master a field from the many who simply work at a job. Our levels of desire, patience, persistence, and confidence end up playing a much larger role in success than sheer reasoning powers.

In the past, only elites or those with an almost superhuman amount of energy and drive could pursue a career of their choice and master it. A man was born into the military, or groomed for the government, chosen among those of the right class. If he happened to display a talent and desire for such work it was mostly a coincidence. Millions of people who were not part of the right social class, gender, and ethnic group were rigidly excluded from the possibility of pursuing their calling. Even if people wanted to follow their inclinations, access to the information and knowledge pertaining to that particular field was controlled by elites. That is why there are relatively few Masters in the past and why they stand out so much.

These social and political barriers, however, have mostly disappeared. Today we have the kind of access to information and knowledge that past Masters could only dream about. Now more than ever, we have the capacity and freedom to move toward the inclination that all of us possess.

Although we may find ourselves at a historical moment rich in possibilities for mastery, in which more and more people can move toward their inclinations, we in fact face one last obstacle in attaining such power, one that is cultural and insidiously dangerous: The very concept of mastery has become denigrated, associated with something old-fashioned and even unpleasant. It is generally not seen as something to aspire to.

Anything that smacks of discipline or effort seems fussy and passé: "Why bother working for years to attain mastery when we can have so much power with very little effort? Technology will solve everything." This passive attitude has even assumed a moral stance: "mastery and power are evil; they are the domain of patriarchal elites."

If you are not careful, you will find this attitude infecting you in subtle ways. You will unconsciously lower your sights as to what you can accomplish in life. This can diminish your levels of effort and discipline below the point of effectiveness. Conforming to social norms, you will listen more to others than to your own voice. You may choose a career path based on what peers and parents tell you, or on what seems lucrative. If you lose contact with this inner calling, you can have some success in life, but eventually your lack of true desire catches up with you. Your work becomes mechanical. You come to live for leisure and immediate pleasures. In this way you become increasingly passive, and never move past the first phase. You may grow frustrated and depressed, never realizing that the source of it is your alienation from your own creative potential.

Before it is too late you must find your way to your inclination, exploiting the incredible opportunities of the age that you have been born into. You must convince yourself of the following: people get the mind and quality of brain that they deserve through their actions in life. Recent discoveries in neuroscience are overturning long-held beliefs that the brain is genetically hardwired. Scientists are demonstrating the degree to which the brain is actually quite plastic—how our thoughts determine our mental landscape. They are exploring the relationship of willpower to physiology, how profoundly the mind can affect our health and functionality. It is possible that more and more will be discovered about how deeply we create the various patterns of our lives through certain mental operations—how we are truly responsible for so much of what happens to us.

People who are passive create a mental landscape that is rather barren. Because of their limited experiences and action, all kinds of connections in the brain die off from lack of use. Pushing against the passive trend of these times, you must work to see how far you can extend control of your circumstances and create the kind of mind you desire—not through drugs but through action. Unleashing the masterful mind within, you will be at the vanguard of those who are exploring the extended limits of human willpower.

In many ways, the movement from one level of intelligence to another can be considered as a kind of ritual of transformation. As you progress, old ideas and perspectives die off; as new powers are unleashed, you are initiated into higher levels of seeing the world. Consider *Mastery* as an invaluable tool in guiding you through this transformative process. The book is designed to lead you from the lowest levels to the highest.

The ideas in the book are based on extensive research in the fields of neuro- and cognitive science, studies on creativity, as well as the biographies of the greatest Masters in history, and interviews with contemporary Masters as well.

The structure of *Mastery* is simple. There are six chapters, moving sequentially through the process. Chapter 1 is the starting point—discovering your calling, your Life's Task. Chapters 2, 3, and 4 discuss different elements of the Apprenticeship Phase (learning skills, working with mentors, acquiring social intelligence). Chapter 5 is devoted to the Creative-Active Phase, and chapter 6 to the ultimate goal—Mastery. Each chapter begins with the story of an iconic historical figure who exemplifies the chapter's overall concept. The section that follows, Keys to Mastery, gives you a detailed analysis of the phase involved, concrete ideas on how to apply this knowledge to your circumstances, and the mind-set that is necessary to fully exploit these ideas. Following the Keys is a section detailing the various strategies you can use to help advance you through the process. These strategies are designed to give you an even greater sense of the practical application of the ideas in the book.

Finally, you must not see this process of moving through levels of intelligence as merely linear, heading toward some kind of ultimate destination known as mastery. Your whole life is a kind of apprenticeship to which you apply your learning skills. Everything that happens to you is a form of instruction if you pay attention. The creativity that you gain in learning a skill so deeply must be constantly refreshed, as you keep forcing your mind back to a state of openness. Even knowledge of your vocation must be revisited throughout the course of your life as changes in circumstance force you to adapt its direction.

In moving toward mastery, you are bringing your mind closer to reality and to life itself. Anything that is alive is in a continual state of change and movement. The moment that you rest, thinking that you have attained the level you desire, a part of your mind enters a phase of decay. You lose your hard-earned creativity and others begin to sense it. This is a power and intelligence that must be continually renewed or it will die.

I

DISCOVER YOUR CALLING: THE LIFE'S TASK

You possess a kind of inner force that seeks to guide you toward your Life's Task—what you are meant to accomplish in the time that you have to live. In childhood this force was clear to you. It directed you toward activities and subjects that fit your natural inclinations. In the intervening years, the force tends to fade in and out as you listen more to parents and peers. The first move toward mastery is always inward— learning who you really are and reconnecting with that innate force. Knowing it with clarity, you will find your way to the proper career path and everything else will fall into place.

THE HIDDEN FORCE

Toward the end of April 1519, after months of illness, the artist Leonardo da Vinci felt certain that his death was only a few days away. For the past two years Leonardo had been living in the château of Cloux in France, the personal guest of the French king, François I. The king had showered him with money and honors, considering him the living embodiment of the Italian Renaissance, which he had wanted to import to France. Leonardo had been most useful to the king, advising him on all kinds of important matters. But now, at the age of sixty-seven, his life was about to end and his thoughts turned toward other things. He made out his will, received the holy sacrament in church, and then returned to his bed, waiting for the end to come.

As he lay there, several of his friends—including the king—visited him. They noticed that Leonardo was in a particularly reflective mood. He was not someone who usually liked to talk about himself, but now he shared memories from his childhood and youth, dwelling on the strange and improbable course of his life.

Leonardo had always had a strong sense of fate, and for years he had been haunted by one particular question: is there some kind of force from within that makes all living things grow and transform themselves? If such a force in nature existed, he wanted to discover it, and he looked for signs of it in every thing he examined. It was an obsession. Now, in his final hours, after his friends had left him alone, Leonardo would have almost certainly applied this question in some form or another to the riddle of his own life, searching for signs of a force or a fate that had brought about his own development and guided him to the present.

Leonardo would have begun such a search by first thinking back to his childhood in the village of Vinci, some twenty miles outside Florence. His father, Ser Piero da Vinci, was a notary and staunch member of the powerful bourgeoisie, but since Leonardo had been born out of wedlock, he was barred from attending the university or practicing any of the noble professions. His schooling therefore was minimal, and so as a child Leonardo was left mostly to himself. He liked most of all to wander through the olive groves around Vinci or to follow a particular path that led to a much different part of the landscape—dense forests full of wild boar, waterfalls cascading over fast-moving streams, swans gliding through pools, strange wildflowers growing out of the sides of cliffs. The intense variety of life in these forests enthralled him.

One day, sneaking into his father's office, he grabbed some sheets of paper—a rather rare commodity in those days, but as a notary his father had a large supply. He took the sheets on his walk into the forest, and sitting upon a rock he began to sketch the various sights around him. He kept returning day after day to do more of the same; even when the weather was bad, he would sit under some kind of shelter and sketch. He had no teachers, no paintings to look at; he did everything by eye, with nature as the model. He noticed that in drawing things he had to observe them much more closely and catch the details that made them come to life.

Once he sketched a white iris, and in observing it so closely he was struck by its peculiar shape. The iris begins as a seed, and then it proceeds through various stages, all of which he had drawn over the past few years. What makes this plant develop through its stages and culminate in this magnificent flower, so unlike any other? Perhaps it possesses a force that pushes it through these various transformations. He would wonder about the metamorphosis of flowers for years to come.

Alone on his deathbed, Leonardo would have thought back to his earliest years as an apprentice in the studio of the Florentine artist Andrea del Verrocchio. He had been admitted there at the age of fourteen because of the remarkable quality of his drawings. Verrocchio instructed his apprentices in all of the sciences that were necessary to produce the work of his studio—engineering, mechanics, chemistry, and metallurgy. Leonardo was eager to learn all of these skills, but soon he discovered in himself something else: he could not simply do an assignment; he needed to make it something of his own, to invent rather than imitate the Master.

One time, as part of his studio work, he was asked to paint an angel in a larger biblical scene designed by Verrocchio. He had decided that he would make his portion of the scene come to life in his own way. In the foreground in front of the angel he painted a flowerbed, but instead of the usual generalized renderings of plants,

Leonardo depicted the flower specimens that he had studied in such detail as a child, with a kind of scientific rigor no one had seen before. For the angel's face, he experimented with his paints and mixed a new blend that gave it a kind of soft radiance that expressed the angel's sublime mood. (To help capture this mood, Leonardo had spent time in the local church observing those in fervent prayer, the expression of one young man serving as the model for the angel.) And finally, he determined that he would be the first artist to create realistic angelic wings.

For this purpose, he went to the marketplace and purchased several birds. He spent hours sketching their wings, how exactly they merged into their bodies. He wanted to create the sensation that these wings had organically grown from the angel's shoulders and would bring it natural flight. As usual, Leonardo could not stop there. After his work was completed he became obsessed with birds, and the idea brewed in his mind that perhaps a human could really fly, if Leonardo could figure out the science behind avian flight. Now, several hours every week, he read and studied everything he could about birds. This was how his mind naturally worked—one idea flowed into another.

Leonardo would certainly have recalled the lowest point in his life—the year 1481. The Pope asked Lorenzo de' Medici to recommend to him the finest artists in Florence to decorate a chapel he just had built, the Sistine Chapel. Lorenzo complied and sent to Rome all of the best Florentine artists, excluding Leonardo. They had never really gotten along. Lorenzo was a literary type, steeped in the classics. Leonardo could not read Latin and had little knowledge of the ancients. He had a more scientific bent to his nature. But at the root of Leonardo's bitterness at this snub was something else— he had come to hate the dependence forced upon artists to gain royal favor, to live from commission to commission. He had grown tired of Florence and the court politics that reigned there.

He made a decision that would change everything in his life: He would establish himself in Milan, and he would devise a new strategy for his livelihood. He would be more than an artist. He would pursue all of the crafts and sciences that interested him—architecture, military engineering, hydraulics, anatomy, sculpture. For any prince or patron that wanted him, he could serve as an overall adviser and artist, for a nice stipend. His mind, he decided, worked best when he had several different projects at hand, allowing him to build all kinds of connections between them.

Reflecting on his life in this way, he would have clearly detected the workings of some kind of hidden force within him. As a child this force had drawn him to the wildest part of the landscape, where he could observe the most intense and dramatic variety of life. This same force compelled him to steal paper from his father and devote his time to sketching. It pushed him to experiment while working for Verrocchio. It guided him away from the courts of Florence and the insecure egos that flourished among artists. It compelled him to an extreme of boldness—the gigantic sculptures, the attempt to fly, the dissection of hundreds of corpses for his anatomical studies—all to discover the essence of life itself.

Seen from this vantage point, everything in his life made sense. It was in fact a blessing to have been born illegitimate—it allowed him to develop in his own way. Even the paper in his house seemed to indicate some kind of destiny. What if he had rebelled against this force? What if, after the Sistine Chapel rejection, he had insisted on going to Rome with the others and forced his way into the Pope's good graces instead of seeking his own path? He was capable of that. What if he had devoted himself to mostly painting in order to make a good living? What if he had been more like the others, finishing his works as fast as possible? He would have done well, but he would not have been Leonardo da Vinci. His life would have lacked the purpose that it had, and inevitably things would have gone wrong.

This hidden force within him, like that within the iris he had sketched so many years before, had led to the full flowering of his capacities. He had faithfully followed its guidance to the very end and, having completed his course, now it was time to die. Perhaps his own words, written years before in his notebook, would have come back to him in such a moment: "Just as a well-filled day brings blessed sleep, so a well-employed life brings a blessed death."

KEYS TO MASTERY

Many of the greatest Masters in history have confessed to experiencing some kind of force or voice or sense of destiny that has guided them forward. Such feelings can be seen as purely mystical, beyond explanation, or as hallucinations and delusions. But there is another way to see them—as eminently real, practical, and explicable. It can be explained in the following way:

All of us are born unique. This uniqueness is marked genetically in our DNA. We are a one-time phenomenon in the universe—our exact genetic makeup has never occurred before nor will it ever be repeated. For all of us, this uniqueness first expresses itself in childhood through certain primal inclinations. For Leonardo it was exploring the natural world around his village and bringing it to life on paper in his own way. For others, it can be an early attraction to visual patterns—often an indication of a future interest in mathematics. Or it can be an attraction to particular physical movements or spatial arrangements. How can we explain such inclinations? They are *forces* within us that come from a deeper place than conscious words can express.

This primal uniqueness naturally wants to assert and express itself, but some experience it more strongly than others. With Masters it is so strong that it feels like something that has its own external reality—a force, a voice, destiny. In moments when we engage in an activity that corresponds to our deepest inclinations, we might experience a touch of this: We feel as if the words we write or the physical movements we perform come so quickly and easily that they are coming from outside us. We are literally "inspired," the Latin word meaning something from the outside breathing within us.

Let us state it in the following way: At your birth a seed is planted. That seed is your uniqueness. It wants to grow, transform itself, and flower to its full potential. It has a natural, assertive energy to it. Your Life's Task is to bring that seed to flower, to express your uniqueness through your work. You have a destiny to fulfill. The stronger you feel and maintain it—as a force, a voice, or in whatever form—the greater your chance for fulfilling this Life's Task and achieving mastery.

What weakens this force, what makes you not feel it or even doubt its existence, is the degree to which you have succumbed to another force in life—social pressures to conform. This *counterforce* can be very powerful. You want to fit into a group. Unconsciously, you might feel that what makes you different is embarrassing or painful. Your parents often act as a counter-force as well. They may seek to direct you to a career path that is lucrative and comfortable. If these counterforces become strong enough, you can lose complete contact with your uniqueness, with who you really are. Your inclinations and desires become modeled on those of others.

This can set you off on a very dangerous path. You end up choosing a career that does not really suit you. Your desire and interest slowly wane and your work suffers for it. You come to see pleasure and fulfillment as something that comes from outside your work. Because you are increasingly less engaged in your career, you fail to pay attention to changes going on in the field—you fall behind the times and pay a price for this. At moments when you must make important decisions, you flounder or follow what others are doing because you have no sense of inner direction or radar to guide you. You have broken contact with your destiny as formed at birth.

At all cost you must avoid such a fate. The process of following your Life's Task all the way to mastery can essentially begin at any point in life. The hidden force within you is always there and ready to be engaged.

The process of realizing your Life's Task comes in three stages: First, you must connect or reconnect with your inclinations, that sense of uniqueness. The first step then is always inward. You search the past for signs of that inner voice or force. You clear away the other voices that might confuse you—parents and peers. You look for an underlying pattern, a core to your character that you must understand as deeply as possible.

Second, with this connection established, you must look at the career path you are already on or are about to begin. The choice of this path—or redirection of it—is critical. To help in this stage you will need to enlarge your concept of work itself.

You want to see your work as something more inspiring, as part of your *vocation*. The word "vocation" comes from the Latin meaning to call or to be called. Its use in relation to work began in early Christianity— certain people were called to a life in the church; that was their vocation. They could recognize this literally by hearing a voice from God, who had chosen them for this profession.

The voice in this case that is calling you is not necessarily coming from God, but from deep within. It emanates from your individuality. It tells you which activities suit your character. And at a certain point, it calls you to a particular form of work or career. Your work then is something connected deeply to who you are.

Finally, you must see your career or vocational path more as a journey with twists and turns rather than a straight line. You begin by choosing a field or position that roughly corresponds to your inclinations. This initial position offers you room to maneuver and important skills to learn. You don't want to start with something too lofty, too ambitious—you need to make a living and establish some confidence. Once on this path you discover certain side routes that attract you, while other aspects of this field leave you cold. You adjust and perhaps move to a related field, continuing to learn more about yourself, but always expanding off your skill base. Like Leonardo, you take what you do for others and make it your own.

Eventually, you will hit upon a particular field, niche, or opportunity that suits you perfectly. You will recognize it when you find it because it will spark that childlike sense of wonder and excitement; it will feel right. Once found, everything will fall into place. You will learn more quickly and more deeply. Your skill level will reach a point where you will be able to claim your independence from within the group you work for and move out on your own. You will determine your circumstances. As your own Master, you will no longer be subject to the whims of tyrannical bosses or scheming peers.

This emphasis on your uniqueness and a Life's Task might seem a poetic conceit without any bearing on practical realities, but in fact it is extremely relevant to the times that we live in. We are entering a world in which we can rely less and less upon the state, the corporation, or family or friends to help and protect us. It is a globalized, harshly competitive environment. We must learn to develop ourselves. At the same time, it is a world teeming with critical problems and opportunities, best solved and seized by entrepreneurs—individuals or small groups who think independently, adapt quickly, and possess unique perspectives. Your individualized, creative skills will be at a premium.

You are born with a particular makeup and tendencies that mark you as a piece of fate. It is who you are to the core. Some people never become who they are; they stop trusting in themselves; they conform to the tastes of others, and they end up wearing a mask that hides their true nature. If you allow yourself to learn who you really are by paying attention to that voice and force within you, then you can become what you were fated to become—an individual, a Master.

STRATEGIES FOR FINDING YOUR LIFE'S TASK

It might seem that connecting to something as personal as your inclinations and Life's Task would be relatively simple and natural, once you recognize their importance. But in fact it is the opposite. It requires a good deal of planning and strategizing to do it properly, since so many obstacles will present themselves. The following five strategies are designed to deal with the main obstacles in your path over time. Pay attention to all of them because you will almost inevitably encounter each one in some form.

1. Return to your origins—The primal inclination strategy

In order to master a field, you must love the subject and feel a profound connection to it. Your interest must transcend the field itself and border on the religious. It is not just physics that interests you, but discovering something about the invisible forces that govern the universe; it is not just film or music that you pursue, but the chance to bring something powerful to life, to give voice to the deepest emotions within you. You will find early signs of these larger, religious-like interests in your childhood, in the form of certain inclinations or attractions that are hard to put into words and are more like sensations— that of deep wonder in pondering a particular question, sensual pleasure or power in engaging in a particular activity. The importance of recognizing these preverbal inclinations is that they are clear indications of an attraction that is not infected by the desires of other people. They are not something embedded in you by your parents, which come with a more superficial connection, something more verbal and conscious. Coming instead from somewhere deeper, they can only be your own, reflections of your unique chemistry.

As you become more sophisticated, you often lose touch with these signals from your primal core. They can be buried beneath all of the other subjects you have studied. Your power and future can depend on reconnecting with this core and returning to your origins. You must dig for signs of such inclinations in your earliest years. Look for its traces in visceral reactions to something simple; a desire to repeat an activity that you never tired of; a subject that stimulated an unusual degree of curiosity; feelings of power attached to particular actions. It is already there within you. You have nothing to create; you merely need to dig and refind what has been buried inside of you all along. If you reconnect with this core at any age, some element of that primitive attraction will spark back to life, indicating a path that can ultimately become your Life's Task.

2. Occupy the perfect niche—The Darwinian strategy

The career world is like an ecological system: People occupy particular fields within which they must compete for resources and survival. The more people there are crowded into a space, the harder it becomes to thrive there. Working in such a field will tend to wear you out as you struggle to get attention, to play the political games, to win scarce resources for yourself. You spend so much time at these games that you have little time left over for true mastery. You are seduced into such fields because you see others there making a living, treading the familiar path. You are not aware of how difficult such a life can be.

The game you want to play is different: to instead find a niche in the ecology that you can dominate. It is never a simple process to find such a niche. It requires patience and a particular strategy. In the beginning you choose a field that roughly corresponds to your interests (medicine, electrical engineering, writing). From there you can go in one of two directions. The first is the narrowing path. From within your chosen field, you look for side paths that particularly attract you (neuroscience, robotics, film writing). When it is possible, you make a move to this narrower field. You continue this process until you eventually hit upon a totally unoccupied niche, the narrower the better. In some ways, this niche corresponds to your uniqueness, to what sets you apart from others.

The second is the connecting–widening path. Once you have mastered your first field, you look for other subjects or skills that you can conquer, on your own time if necessary. You can now combine this added field of knowledge to the original one, perhaps creating a new field, or at least making novel connections between them. You continue this process as long as you wish. Ultimately you create a field that is uniquely your own. This second version fits in well with a culture where information is so widely available, and in which connecting ideas is a form of power.

In either direction, you have found a niche that is not crowded with competitors. You have freedom to roam, to pursue particular questions that interest you. You set your own agenda and command the resources available to this niche. Unburdened by overwhelming competition and politicking, you have time and space to bring to flower your Life's Task.

3. Avoid the false path—The rebellion strategy

A false path in life is generally a career we are attracted to for the wrong reasons—money, fame, attention, and so on. If it is attention we need, we often experience a kind of emptiness inside that we are hoping to fill with the false love of public approval. Because the field we choose does not correspond with our deepest inclinations, we rarely find the fulfillment that we crave. Our work suffers for this, and the attention we may have gotten in the beginning starts to fade—a painful process. If it is money and comfort that dominate our decision, we are most often acting out of anxiety and the need to please our parents. They may steer us toward something lucrative out of care and concern, but lurking underneath this can be something else—perhaps a bit of envy that we have more freedom than they had when they were young.

If this happens to you, your strategy must be two-fold: first, to realize as early as possible that you have chosen your career for the wrong reasons, before your confidence takes a hit. And second, to actively rebel against those forces that have pushed you away from your true path. Scoff at the need for attention and approval—they will lead you astray. Feel some anger and resentment at the parental forces that want to foist upon you an alien vocation. It is a healthy part of your development to follow a path independent of your parents and to establish your own identity. Let your sense of rebellion fill you with energy and purpose.

4. Let go of the past—The adaptation strategy

In dealing with your career and its inevitable changes, you must think in the following way: You are not tied to a particular position; your loyalty is not to a career or a company. You are committed to your Life's Task, to giving it full expression. It is up to you to find it and guide it correctly. It is not up to others to protect or help you. You are on your own. Change is inevitable, particularly in such a revolutionary moment as ours. Since you are on your own, it is up to you to foresee the changes going on right now in your profession. You must adapt your Life's Task to these circumstances. You do not hold on to past ways of doing things, because that will ensure you will fall behind and suffer for it. You are flexible and always looking to adapt.

If change is forced upon you, you must resist the

temptation to overreact or feel sorry for yourself. Instead, you must look to find a way to adapt your experience, interests and inclinations to a new direction. You don't want to abandon the skills and experience you have gained, but to find a new way to apply them. Your eye is on the future, not the past. Often such creative readjustments lead to a superior path for us—we are shaken out of our complacency and forced to reassess where we are headed. Remember: your Life's Task is a living, breathing organism. The moment you rigidly follow a plan set in your youth, you lock yourself into a position, and the times will ruthlessly pass you by.

5. Find your way back—The life-or-death strategy

No good can ever come from deviating from the path that you were destined to follow. You will be assailed by varieties of hidden pain. Most often you deviate because of the lure of money, of more immediate prospects of prosperity. Because this does not comply with something deep within you, your interest will lag and eventually the money will not come so easily. You will search for other easy sources of money, moving further and further away from your path. Not seeing clearly ahead of you, you will end up in a dead-end career. Even if your material needs are met, you will feel an emptiness inside that you will need to fill with any kind of belief system, drugs, or diversions. There is no compromise here, no way of escaping the dynamic. You will recognize how far you have deviated by the depth of your pain and frustration. You must listen to the message of this frustration, this pain, and let it guide you. It is a matter of life and death.

The way back requires a sacrifice. You cannot have everything in the present. The road to mastery requires patience. You will have to keep your focus on five or ten years down the road, when you will reap the rewards of your efforts. The process of getting there, however, is full of challenges and pleasures. Make your return to the path a resolution you set for yourself, and then tell others about it. It becomes a matter of shame and embarrassment to deviate from this path. In the end, the money and success that truly last come not to those who focus on such things as goals, but rather to those who focus on mastery and fulfilling their Life's Task.

II

SUBMIT TO REALITY: THE IDEAL APPRENTICESHIP

After your formal education, you enter the most critical phase in your life—a second, practical education known as The Apprenticeship. The dangers are many. If you are not careful, you will succumb to insecurities, become embroiled in emotional issues and conflicts that will dominate your thoughts; you will develop fears and learning disabilities that you will carry with you throughout your life. Before it is too late you must learn the lessons and follow the path established by the greatest Masters, past and present—a kind of Ideal Apprenticeship that transcends all fields.

THE FIRST TRANSFORMATION

From early in his life, Charles Darwin (1809–82) felt the presence of his father bearing down on him. The father was a successful and wealthy country doctor who had high hopes for his two sons. But Charles, the youngest, seemed to be the one who was less likely to meet his expectations. He was not good at Greek and Latin, or algebra, or really anything in school. It wasn't that he lacked ambition. It was just that learning about the world through books did not interest him. He loved the outdoors—hunting, scouring the countryside for rare breeds of beetles, collecting flower and mineral specimens. He could spend hours observing the behavior of birds and taking elaborate notes on their various differences. He had an eye for such things. But these hobbies did not add up to a career, and as he got older he could sense his father's growing impatience. One day, his father rebuked him with words Charles would never forget: "You care for nothing but shooting, dogs, and rat-catching, and you will be a disgrace to yourself and all your family."

When Charles turned fifteen, his father decided to become more actively involved in his life. He sent him off to medical school in Edinburgh, but Charles could not stand the sight of blood and so had to drop out. Determined to find some career for him, the father then secured for his son a future position in the church as a country parson. For this Charles would be well paid, and he would have plenty of spare time to pursue his mania for collecting specimens. The only requirement for such a position was a degree from an eminent university, and so Charles was enrolled at Cambridge. Once again, he had to confront his disinterest in formal schooling. He tried his best. He developed an interest in botany and became good friends with his instructor, Professor Henslow. He worked as hard as he could, and to his father's relief he managed, barely, to earn his Bachelor of Arts in May 1831.

Hoping that his schooling was forever over, Charles left on a tour of the English countryside where he could indulge in all of his passions for the outdoors and forget about the future, for the time being.

When he returned home in late August, he was surprised to see a letter waiting for him from Professor Henslow. The professor was recommending Charles for a position as an unpaid naturalist on the HMS *Beagle*, which was to leave in a few months on a several-year journey around the globe, surveying various coastlines. As part of his job, Charles would be in charge of collecting life and mineral specimens along the way and sending them back to England for examination. Evidently, Henslow had been impressed by the young man's remarkable skill in collecting and identifying plant specimens.

This offer confused Charles. He had never thought of traveling that far, let alone pursuing a career as a naturalist. Before he really had time to consider it, his father weighed in—he was dead set against his accepting the offer. Charles had never been to sea and would not take to it well. He was not a trained scientist, and lacked the discipline. Moreover, taking several years on this voyage would jeopardize the position his father had secured for him in the church.

His father was so forceful and persuasive that Charles could not help but agree, and he decided to turn the offer down. But over the next few days he thought about this voyage and what it could be like. And the more he imagined it, the more it appealed to him. Perhaps it was the lure of adventure after leading such a sheltered childhood, or the chance to explore a possible career as a naturalist, seeing along the way almost every possible life form the planet could offer. Or maybe he needed to get away from his overbearing father and find his own way. Whatever the reason, he soon decided that he had changed his mind and wanted to accept the offer. Recruiting an uncle to his cause, he managed to get his father to give his very reluctant consent. On the eve of the ship's departure, Charles wrote to the captain of the *Beagle*, Robert FitzRoy: "My second life will then commence, and it shall be as a birthday for the rest of my life."

The ship set sail in December of that year and almost instantly young Darwin regretted his decision. The boat was rather small and strongly buffeted by the waves. He was continually seasick and could not hold his food. His heart ached at the thought that he would not see his family for so long, and that he would have to spend so many years cooped up with all of these strangers. He developed heart palpitations and felt like he was dangerously ill. The sailors sensed his lack of seaworthiness and eyed him strangely. Captain FitzRoy proved to be a man of wildly swinging moods, suddenly turning furious over the most seemingly trivial events. He was also a religious fanatic who believed in the literal truth of the Bible; it was Darwin's duty, FitzRoy told him, to find in South America evidence of the Flood and the creation of life as described in Genesis. Darwin felt like a fool for going against his father, and his sense of loneliness was crushing. How could he endure this cramped existence for months on end, living in close quarters with a captain who seemed half-insane?

A few weeks into the journey, feeling somewhat desperate, he decided upon a strategy. Whenever he experienced such inner turmoil at home, what always calmed him down was to head outdoors and observe the life around him. In that way he could forget himself. This now was his world. He would observe life on board this ship, the characters of the various sailors and the captain himself, as if he were taking note of the markings of butterflies. For instance, he noticed that no one grumbled about the food or the weather or the tasks at hand. They valued stoicism. He would try to adopt such an attitude. It seemed that FitzRoy was slightly insecure and needed constant validation about his authority and high position within the navy. Darwin would supply that to no end. Slowly, he began to fit into the daily scheme of life. He even picked up some of the mannerisms of the sailors. All of this distracted him from his loneliness.

Several months later the *Beagle* arrived in Brazil,

and now Darwin understood why he had wanted so badly to go on this voyage. He was completely mesmerized by the intense variety of the vegetation and wildlife—this was a naturalist's paradise. It was not like anything he had observed or collected in England. One day on a walk through a forest, he stood to the side and witnessed the most bizarre and cruel spectacle he had ever seen: a march of tiny black ants, their columns over a hundred yards long, devouring every living thing in their path. Everywhere he turned he saw some example of the fierce struggle for survival in forests with overabundant life. In attending to his work, he quickly realized that he also faced a problem: All of the birds, the butterflies, the crabs, and the spiders he caught were so unusual. Part of his job was to choose judiciously what to send back, but how could he possibly distinguish what was worth collecting?

He would have to expand his knowledge. Not only would he have to spend endless hours studying everything in his sight on his walks, and take copious notes, but he would have to find a way to organize all of this information, catalog all of these specimens, bring some order to his observations. It would be a herculean task, but unlike schoolwork, it excited him. These were living creatures, not vague notions in books.

As the ship headed south along the coast, Darwin realized that there were interior parts of South America that no naturalist had yet explored. Determined to see every form of life that he could possibly find, he began a series of treks into the Pampas of Argentina, accompanied only by gauchos, collecting all kinds of unusual animal and insect specimens. Adopting the same strategy as on the ship, he observed the gauchos and their ways, fitting into their culture as if one of them. On these and other jaunts, he would brave marauding Indians, poisonous insects, and jaguars lurking in the forests. Without thinking of it, he had developed a taste for adventure that would have shocked his family and friends.

A year into the voyage, on a beach some 400 miles south of Buenos Aires, Darwin discovered something that would set his mind to thinking for many years to come. He came upon a cliff with streaks of white amid the rock. Seeing that they were enormous bones of some sort, he began to chip away at the rock, extracting as many of these remains as possible. They were of a size and kind he had never seen before—the horns and armor of what seemed to be a giant armadillo, the huge teeth of a mastodon, and then, most surprisingly, the tooth of a horse. When the Spaniards and Portuguese had first arrived in South America there were no horses to be found, and yet this tooth was quite old and predated their arrival. He began to wonder—if such species had died off long ago, the idea of all of life being created at once and for good seemed illogical. More important, how could so many species become extinct? Could life on the planet be in a state of constant flux and development?

Months later he was trekking through the high Andes, looking for rare geological specimens to send back. At an elevation of about 12,000 feet he discovered some fossilized seashells and deposits of marine rocks—a rather surprising find at such an altitude. As he examined them and the surrounding flora, he speculated that these mountains had once stood in the Atlantic Ocean. A series of volcanoes, thousands of years ago, must have raised them higher and higher. Instead of relics to support the stories in the Bible, he was finding evidence for something shockingly different.

As the journey progressed, Darwin noted some obvious changes in himself. He used to find almost any kind of work boring, but now he could labor all hours of the day; in fact, with so much to explore and learn, he hated wasting a single minute of the voyage. He had cultivated an incredible eye for the flora and fauna of South America. He could identify local birds by their songs, the markings on their eggs, their manner of taking flight. All of this information he could catalog and organize in an efficient manner. More important, his whole way of thinking had changed. He would observe something, read and write about it, then develop a theory after even more observation, the theories and observations feeding off one another. Full of details about so many facets of the world he was exploring, ideas were sprouting up out of nowhere.

In September 1835, the *Beagle* left the Pacific Coast of South America and headed west for the journey home. Their first stop along the way was a series of virtually unoccupied islands known as the Galápagos. The islands were famous for their wildlife, but nothing could prepare Darwin for what he would find there. Captain FitzRoy gave him one week to explore one of the islands, and then they would be on their way. From the moment he stepped on the island, Darwin realized something was different: this small speck of land was crammed with life that was not like anywhere else—thousands of black marine iguanas swarming around him, on the beach and in the shallow water; 500-pound tortoises lumbering about the shore; seals, penguins, and flightless cormorants, all cold-water creatures, inhabiting a tropical island.

By the end of the week, he had counted twenty-six unique species of land birds on this one island alone. His jars began to fill up with the most bizarre plants, snakes, lizards, fish, and insects. Back on board the *Beagle*, he began to catalog and categorize the remarkable number of specimens he had collected. He was struck by the fact that almost all of them represented completely new species. He then made an even more remarkable discovery: the species differed from island to island, even though they were only some fifty miles apart. The tortoise shells had different markings, and the finches had developed different types of beaks, each designed for a specific kind of food on their particular island.

Suddenly, as if the four years of this voyage and all of his observations had distilled in him a deeper way of thinking, a radical theory took shape in his mind: These islands, he speculated, had first been pushed up out of the water by volcanic eruptions, much like the Andes. In the beginning, there was no life to be found on them.

Slowly, birds visited and deposited seeds. Various animals arrived by sea—lizards or insects floating on logs; tortoises, originally of a marine variety, swam over. Over thousands of years, each creature adapted to the food and predators that were found there, changing their shape and appearance in the process. Animals that failed to adapt died out, like the fossils of those giant creatures Darwin had unearthed in Argentina. It was a ruthless struggle for survival. Life was not created on these islands at one time and for good by some divine being. The creatures here had ever so slowly evolved to their present form. And these islands represented a microcosm of the planet itself.

On the journey home Darwin began to develop this theory further, so revolutionary in its implications. To prove his theory would now be his life's work.

Finally, in October 1836, the *Beagle* returned to England after nearly five years at sea. Darwin hurried home, and when his father first saw him he was astonished. Physically, he had changed. His head seemed larger. His whole manner was different—a seriousness of purpose and sharpness could be read in his eyes, almost the opposite look of the lost young man who had gone to sea years before. Clearly, the voyage had transformed his son in body and spirit.

KEYS TO MASTERY

One can have no smaller or greater mastery than mastery of oneself.

—Leonardo da Vinci

In the stories of the greatest Masters, past and present, we can inevitably detect a phase in their lives in which all of their future powers were in development, like the chrysalis of a butterfly. This part of their lives—a largely self-directed apprenticeship that lasts some five to ten years—receives little attention because it does not contain stories of great achievement or discovery. Often in their Apprenticeship Phase, these types are not yet much different from anyone else. Under the surface, however, their minds are transforming in ways we cannot see but contain all of the seeds of their future success.

Much of how such Masters navigate this phase comes from an intuitive grasp of what is most important and essential for their development, but in studying what they did right we can learn some invaluable lessons for ourselves. In fact, a close examination of their lives reveals a pattern that transcends their various fields, indicating a kind of *Ideal Apprenticeship* for mastery. And to grasp this pattern, to follow it in our own ways, we must understand something about the very idea and necessity for passing through an apprenticeship.

In childhood we are inculcated in culture through

a long period of dependency—far longer than any other animal. During this period we learn language, writing, math, and reasoning skills, along with a few others. Much of this happens under the watchful and loving guidance of parents and teachers. As we get older, greater emphasis is placed on book learning—absorbing as much information as possible about various subjects. Such knowledge of history, science, or literature is abstract, and the process of learning largely involves passive absorption. At the end of this process (usually somewhere between the ages of eighteen and twenty-five) we are then thrust into the cold, harsh work world to fend for ourselves.

When we emerge from the youthful state of dependency, we are not really ready to handle the transition to an entirely independent phase. We carry with us the habit of learning from books or teachers, which is largely unsuited for the practical, self-directed phase of life that comes next. We tend to be somewhat socially naïve and unprepared for the political games people play. Still uncertain as to our identity, we think that what matters in the work world is gaining attention and making friends. And these misconceptions and naïveté are brutally exposed in the light of the real world.

If we adjust over time, we might eventually find our way; but if we make too many mistakes, we create endless problems for ourselves. We spend too much time entangled in emotional issues, and we never quite have enough detachment to reflect and learn from our experiences. The apprenticeship, by its very nature, must be conducted by each individual in his or her own way. To follow *precisely* the lead of others or advice from a book is self-defeating. This is the phase in life in which we finally declare our independence and establish who we are. But for this second education in our lives, so critical to our future success, there are some powerful and essential lessons that we all can benefit from, that can guide us away from common mistakes and save us valuable time.

These lessons transcend all fields and historical periods because they are connected to something essential about human psychology and how the brain itself functions. They can be distilled into one overarching *principle* for the Apprenticeship Phase, and a process that loosely follows three steps.

The principle is simple and must be engraved deeply in your mind: the goal of an apprenticeship is not money, a good position, a title, or a diploma, but rather the *transformation* of your mind and character—the first transformation on the way to mastery. You enter a career as an outsider. You are naïve and full of misconceptions about this new world. Your head is full of dreams and fantasies about the future. Your knowledge of the world is subjective, based on emotions, insecurities, and limited experience. Slowly, you will ground yourself in reality, in the objective world represented by the knowledge and skills that make people successful in it. You will learn how to work with others and handle criticism. In the process you will transform yourself from someone who is impatient and scattered into someone who is disciplined and focused, with a mind that can handle complexity. In the end, you will master yourself and all of your weaknesses.

This has a simple consequence: you must choose places of work and positions that offer the greatest possibilities for learning. Practical knowledge is the ultimate commodity, and is what will pay you dividends for decades to come—far more than the paltry increase in pay you might receive at some seemingly lucrative position that offers fewer learning opportunities. This means that you move toward challenges that will toughen and improve you, where you will get the most objective feedback on your performance and progress. You do not choose apprenticeships that seem easy and comfortable.

In this sense you must see yourself as following in the footsteps of Charles Darwin. You are finally on your own, on a voyage in which you will craft your own future. It is the time of youth and adventure—of exploring the world with an open mind and spirit. In fact, whenever you must learn a new skill or alter your career path later in life, you reconnect with that youthful, adventurous part of yourself. Darwin could have played it safe, collecting what was necessary, and spending more time on board studying instead of actively exploring. In that case, he would not have become an illustrious scientist, but just another collector. He constantly looked for challenges, pushing himself past his comfort zone. He used danger and difficulties as a way to measure his progress. You must adopt such a spirit and see your apprenticeship as a kind of journey in which you will transform yourself, rather than as a drab indoctrination into the work world.

The Apprenticeship Phase—The Three Steps or Modes

With the *principle* outlined above guiding you in your choices, you must think of three essential steps in your apprenticeship, each one overlapping the other. These steps are: *Deep Observation* (*The Passive Mode*), *Skills Acquisition* (*The Practice Mode*), and *Experimentation* (*The Active Mode*). Keep in mind that an apprenticeship can come in many different forms. It can happen at one place over several years, or it can consist of several different positions in different places.

Step One: Deep Observation—The Passive Mode

When you enter a career or new environment, you move into a world with its own rules, procedures, and social dynamic. For decades or even centuries, people have compiled knowledge of how to get things done in a particular field, each generation improving on the past. In addition, every workplace has its own conventions, rules of behavior, and work standards. There are also all kinds of power relationships that exist between individuals. All of this represents a reality that transcends your individual needs and desires. And so your task upon entering this world is to *observe* and absorb its reality as *deeply* as possible.

The greatest mistake you can make in the initial months of your apprenticeship is to imagine that you have to get attention, impress people, and prove your-self. These thoughts will dominate your mind and close it off from the reality around you. Any positive attention you receive is deceptive; it is not based on your skills or anything real, and it will turn against you. Instead, you will want to acknowledge the reality and *submit* to it, muting your colors and keeping in the background as much as possible, remaining passive and giving yourself the space to observe. You will also want to drop any preconceptions you might have about this world you are entering. If you impress people in these first months, it should be because of the seriousness of your desire to learn, not because you are trying to rise to the top before you are ready.

You will be observing two essential realities in this new world. First, you will observe the rules and pro-cedures that govern success in this environment—in other words, "this is how we do things here." Some of these rules will be communicated to you directly—generally the ones that are superficial and largely a mat-ter of common sense. You must pay attention to these and observe them, but what is of more interest are the rules that are unstated and are part of the underlying work culture. These concern style and values that are considered important. They are often a reflection of the character of the man or woman on top.

You can observe such rules by looking at those who are on their way up in the hierarchy, who have a golden touch. More tellingly, you can observe those who are more awkward, who have been chastised for particular mistakes or even been fired. Such examples serve as negative trip wires: do things this way and you will suffer.

The second reality you will observe is the power relationships that exist within the group: who has real control; through whom do all communications flow; who is on the rise and who is on the decline. These procedural and political rules may be dysfunctional or counterproductive, but your job is not to moralize about this or complain, but merely to understand them, to get a complete lay of the land.

Every task you are given, no matter how menial, offers opportunities to observe this world at work. No detail about the people within it is too trivial. Everything you see or hear is a sign for you to decode. Over time, you will begin to see and understand more of the reality that eluded you at first. As you amass more information about the rules and power dynamics of your new environment, you can begin to analyze why they exist, and how they relate to larger trends in the field. You move from observation to analysis, honing your reasoning skills, but only after months of careful attention.

Understand: there are several critical reasons why you must follow this step. First, knowing your environment inside and out will help you in navigating it and avoiding costly mistakes. You are like a hunter: your knowledge of every detail of the forest and of the ecosystem as a whole will give you many more options for survival and success. Second, the ability to observe any unfamiliar environment will become a critical lifelong skill. You will develop the habit of stilling your ego and looking outward instead of inward. You will see in any encounter what most people miss because they are thinking of themselves. You will cultivate a keen eye for human psychology, and strengthen your ability to focus. Finally, you will become accustomed to observing first, basing your ideas and theories on what you have seen with your eyes, and then analyzing what you find. This will be a very important skill for the next, creative phase in life.

Step Two: Skills Acquisition—The Practice Mode

At some point, as you progress through these initial months of observation, you will enter the most critical part of the apprenticeship: *practice toward the acquisition of skills.* Every human activity, endeavor, or career path involves the mastering of skills. In some fields, it is direct and obvious, like operating a tool or machine or creating something physical. In others, it is more of a mix of the physical and mental, such as the observing and collecting of specimens for Charles Darwin. In still others, the skills are more nebulous, such as handling people or researching and organizing information. As much as possible, you want to reduce these skills to something simple and essential—the core of what you need to get good at, skills that can be practiced.

In acquiring any kind of skill, there exists a natural learning process that coincides with the functioning of our brains. This learning process leads to what we shall call *tacit knowledge*—a feeling for what you are doing that is hard to put into words but easy to demonstrate in action. And to understand how this learning process operates, it is useful to look at the greatest system ever invented for the training of skills and the achievement of tacit knowledge—the apprenticeship system of the Middle Ages, in which young people from approximately the ages of twelve to seventeen would enter work in a shop, signing a contract that would commit them for the term of seven years. At the end of this term, apprentices would have to pass a *master test*, or produce a *master work*, to prove their level of skill.

Because few books or drawings existed at the time, apprentices would learn the trade by watching Masters and imitating them as closely as possible. They learned through endless repetition and hands-on work, with very little verbal instruction. If one added up the time that apprentices ended up working directly on materials in those years, it would amount to more than 10,000 hours, enough to establish exceptional skill level at a craft. The power of this form of tacit knowledge is embodied in the great Gothic cathedrals of Europe—masterpieces of beauty, craftsmanship, and stability, all erected without blueprints or books. These cathedrals represented the accumulated skills of numerous craftsmen and engineers.

What this means is simple: language, oral and written, is a relatively recent invention. Well before that time, our ancestors had to learn various skills—toolmaking, hunting, and so forth. The natural model for learning came from watching and imitating others, then repeating the action over and over. Our brains are highly suited for this form of learning.

Even with skills that are primarily mental, such as computer programming or speaking a foreign language, it remains the case that we learn best through practice and repetition—the natural learning process. We learn a foreign language by actually speaking it as much as possible, not by reading books and absorbing theories. The more we speak and practice, the more fluent we become.

Once you take this far enough, you enter a *cycle of accelerated returns* in which the practice becomes easier and more interesting, leading to the ability to practice for longer hours, which increases your skill level, which in turn makes practice even more interesting. Reaching this cycle is the goal you must set for yourself, and to get there you must understand some basic principles about skills themselves.

First, it is essential that you begin with one skill that you can master, and that serves as a foundation for acquiring others. You must avoid at all cost the idea that you can manage learning several skills at a time. You need to develop your powers of concentration, and understand that trying to multitask will be the death of the process.

Second, the initial stages of learning a skill invariably involve tedium. Yet rather than avoiding this inevitable tedium, you must accept and embrace it. The pain and boredom we experience in the initial stage of learning a skill toughens our minds, much like physical exercise.

Once something is repeated often enough, it becomes hardwired and automatic. This process of hardwiring cannot occur if you are constantly distracted, moving from one task to another. Once an action becomes automatic, you now have the mental space to observe yourself as you practice. You must use this distance to take note of your weaknesses or flaws that need correction—to analyze yourself. It helps also to gain as much feedback as possible from others, to have standards against which you can measure your progress so that you are aware of how far you have to go. Trying something over and over again grounds you in reality, making you deeply aware of your inadequacies and of what you can accomplish with more work and effort.

If you take this far enough, you will naturally enter the cycle of accelerated returns: As elements become more automatic your mind is not exhausted by the effort and you can practice harder, which in turn brings greater skill and more pleasure. You can look for challenges, new areas to conquer, keeping your interest at a high level. As the cycle accelerates, you can reach a point where your mind is totally absorbed in the practice, entering a kind of flow in which everything else is blocked out. You become one with the tool or instrument or thing you are studying.

In essence, when you practice and develop any skill you transform yourself in the process. Your sense of pleasure becomes redefined. What offers immediate pleasure comes to seem like a distraction, an empty entertainment to help pass the time. Real pleasure comes from overcoming challenges, feeling confidence in your abilities, gaining fluency in skills, and experiencing the power this brings.

Although it might seem that the time necessary to master the requisite skills and attain a level of expertise would depend on the field and your own talent level, those who have researched the subject repeatedly come up with the number of 10,000 hours. This seems to be the amount of quality practice time that is needed for someone to reach a high level of skill and it applies to composers, chess players, writers, and athletes, among others. 10,000 hours generally adds up to seven to ten years of sustained, solid practice—roughly the period of a traditional apprenticeship. In other words, concentrated practice over time cannot fail but produce results.

Step Three: Experimentation—The Active Mode

This is the shortest part of the process, but a critical component nonetheless. As you gain in skill and confidence, you must make the move to a more *active* mode of *experimentation*. This could mean taking on more responsibility, initiating a project of some sort, doing work that exposes you to the criticisms of peers or even the public. The point of this is to gauge your progress and whether there are still gaps in your knowledge. You are observing yourself in action and seeing how you respond to the judgments of others. Can you take criticism and use it constructively?

Most people wait too long to take this step, generally out of fear. It is always easier to learn the rules and stay within your comfort zone. Often you must force yourself to initiate such actions or experiments *before you think you are ready.* You are testing your character, moving past your fears, and developing a sense of detachment to your work—looking at it through the eyes of others. You are getting a taste for the next phase in which what you produce will be under constant scrutiny.

You will know when your apprenticeship is over by the feeling that you have nothing left to learn in this environment. It is time to declare your independence or move to another place to continue your apprenticeship and expand your skill base. Later in life, when you are confronted with a career change or the need to learn new skills, having gone through this process before, it will become second nature. You have learned how to learn.

◆

Many people might find the notion of an apprenticeship and skill acquisition as quaint relics of bygone eras when work meant making things. After all, we have entered the information and computer age, in which technology makes it so we can do without the kinds of menial tasks that require practice and repetition; so many things have become virtual in our lives, making the craftsman model obsolete. Or so the argument goes.

In truth, however, the era we have entered is not one in which technology will make everything easier, but rather a time of increased complexity that affects every field. In business, competition has become globalized and more intense. A businessperson must have a command of a much larger picture than in the past, which means more knowledge and skills. The future in science lies in the combining and cross-fertilization of knowledge in various fields. In the arts, tastes and styles are changing at an accelerated rate. An artist must be on top of this and be capable of creating new forms, always remaining ahead of the curve. This often requires having more than just a specialized knowledge of that particular art form—it requires knowing other arts, even the sciences, and what is happening in the world.

In all of these areas, the human brain is asked to do and handle more than ever before. We are dealing with several fields of knowledge constantly intersecting with our own, and all of this chaos is exponentially increased by the information available through technology. What this means is that all of us must possess different forms of knowledge and an array of skills in different fields, and have minds that are capable of organizing large amounts of information. The future belongs to those who learn more skills and combine them in creative ways. And the process of learning skills, no matter how virtual, remains the same.

In the future, the great division will be between those who have trained themselves to handle these complexities and those who are overwhelmed by them—those who can acquire skills and discipline their minds and those who are irrevocably distracted by all the media around them and can never focus enough to learn. The Apprenticeship Phase is more relevant and important than ever, and those who discount this notion will almost certainly be left behind.

STRATEGIES FOR COMPLETING THE IDEAL APPRENTICESHIP

> *Do not think that what is hard for you to master is humanly impossible; and if it is humanly possible, consider it to be within your reach.*
> —Marcus Aurelius

Throughout history, Masters in all fields have devised for themselves various strategies to help them pursue and complete an Ideal Apprenticeship. The following are eight classic strategies, distilled from the stories of their lives. Although some might seem more relevant than others to your circumstances, each of them relates fundamental truths about the learning process itself that you would be wise to internalize.

1. Value learning over money

It is a simple law of human psychology that your thoughts will tend to revolve around what you value most. If it is money, you will choose a place for your apprenticeship that offers the biggest paycheck. Inevitably, in such a place you will feel greater pressures to prove yourself worthy of such pay, often before you are really ready. You will be focused on yourself, your insecurities, the need to please and impress the right people, and not on acquiring skills. It will be too costly for you to make mistakes and learn from them, so you will develop a cautious, conservative approach. As you progress in life, you will become addicted to the fat paycheck and it will determine where you go, how you think, and what you do. Eventually, the time that was not spent on learning skills will catch up with you, and the fall will be painful.

Instead, you must value learning above everything else. This will lead you to all of the right choices. You will opt for the situation that will give you the most opportunities to learn, particularly with hands-on work. You will choose a place that has people and mentors who can inspire and teach you. A job with mediocre pay has the added benefit of training you to get by with less—a valuable life skill. If your apprenticeship is to be mostly on your own time (a self-apprenticeship), you will choose a place that pays the bills—perhaps one that keeps your mind sharp, but that also leaves you the time and mental space to do valuable work on your own. You must never disdain an apprenticeship with no pay. In fact, it is often the height of wisdom to find the perfect mentor and offer your services as an assistant for free. Happy to exploit your cheap and eager spirit, such mentors will often divulge more than the usual trade secrets. In the end, by valuing learning above all else, you will set the stage for your creative expansion, and the money will soon come to you.

2. Keep expanding your horizons

For most people, this is the reality of the Apprenticeship Phase—no one is really going to help you or give you direction in fashioning an apprenticeship. In fact, the odds are against you. If you desire an apprenticeship, if you want to learn and set yourself up for mastery, you have to do it yourself, and with great energy. When you enter this phase, you generally begin at the lowest position. Your access to knowledge and people is limited by your status. If you are not careful, you will accept this status and become defined by it. Instead, you must struggle against any limitations and continually work to expand your horizons. Reading books and materials that go beyond what is required is always a good starting point. Being exposed to ideas in the wide world, you will tend to develop a hunger for more and more knowledge; you will find it harder to remain satisfied in any narrow corner, which is precisely the point. You submit to the reality of being weak and needing to learn what is required, but you place no limits on the subjects you will learn and the skills you will acquire.

The people in your field, in your immediate circle, are like worlds unto themselves—their stories and viewpoints will naturally expand your horizons and build up your social skills. Mingle with as many different types of people as possible. Those circles will slowly widen. Any kind of outside schooling will add to the dynamic. Be relentless in your pursuit for expansion. Whenever you feel like you are settling into some circle, force yourself to shake things up and look for new challenges. With your mind expanding, you will redefine the limits of your apparent world. Soon, ideas and opportunities will come to you and your apprenticeship will naturally complete itself.

3. Revert to a feeling of inferiority

What prevents people from learning is not the subject itself, no matter how difficult it is (the human mind has limitless capabilities), but rather certain learning disabilities that tend to fester and grow in our minds as we get older. These include a sense of smugness and superiority whenever we encounter something alien to our ways, as well as rigid ideas about what is real or true, often indoctrinated in us by schooling or family. If we feel like we know something, our minds close off to other possibilities. We see reflections of the truth we have already assumed. Such feelings of superiority are often unconscious and stem from a fear of what is different or unknown. We are rarely aware of this, and often imagine ourselves to be paragons of impartiality.

Children are generally free of these handicaps. They are dependent upon adults for their survival and naturally feel inferior. This sense of inferiority gives them a hunger to learn. Through learning, they can bridge the gap and not feel so helpless. Their minds are completely open; they pay greater attention. This is why children can learn so quickly and so deeply. Unlike other animals, we humans retain what is known as neoteny—mental and physical traits of immaturity—well into our adult years. We have the remarkable capability of returning to a childlike spirit, especially in moments in which we must learn something. Well into our fifties and beyond, we can return to that sense of wonder and curiosity, reviving our youth and apprenticeships.

Understand: when you enter a new environment, your task is to learn and absorb as much as possible. For that purpose you must try to revert to a childlike feeling of inferiority—the feeling that others know much more than you and that you are dependent upon them to learn and safely navigate your apprenticeship. You drop all of your preconceptions about an environment or field, any lingering feelings of smugness. You have no fears. You interact with people and participate in the culture as deeply as possible. You are full of curiosity. Assuming this sensation of inferiority, your mind will open up and you will have a hunger to learn. This position is of course only temporary. You are reverting to a feeling of dependence, so that within five to ten years you can learn enough to finally declare your independence and enter full adulthood.

4. Trust the process

What separates Masters from others is often something surprisingly simple. Whenever we learn a skill, we frequently reach a point of frustration—what we are learning seems beyond our capabilities. Giving in to these feelings, we unconsciously quit on ourselves before we actually give up. The difference between those who succeed and those who don't is not simply a matter of determination, but more of trust and faith. Many of those who succeed in life have had the experience in their youth of having mastered some skill—a sport or game, a musical instrument, a foreign language, and so on. Buried in their minds is the sensation of overcoming their frustrations and entering the cycle of accelerated returns. In moments of doubt in the present, the memory of the past experience rises to the surface. Filled with trust in the process, they trudge on well past the point at which others slow down or mentally quit.

When it comes to mastering a skill, time is the magic ingredient. Assuming your practice proceeds at a steady level, over days and weeks certain elements of the skill become hardwired. Slowly, the entire skill becomes internalized, part of your nervous system. The mind is no longer mired in the details, but can see the larger picture. It is a miraculous sensation and practice will lead you to that point, no matter the talent level you are born with. The only real impediment to this is yourself and your emotions—boredom, panic, frustration, insecurity. You cannot suppress such emotions—they are normal to the process and are experienced by everyone, including Masters. What you can do is have faith in the process. The boredom will go away once you enter the cycle. The panic disappears after repeated exposure. The frustration is a sign of progress—a signal that your mind is processing complexity and requires more practice. The insecurities will transform into their opposites when you gain mastery. Trusting this will all happen, you will allow the natural learning process to move forward, and everything else will fall into place.

5. Move toward resistance and pain

By nature, we humans shrink from anything that seems possibly painful or overtly difficult. We bring this natural tendency to our practice of any skill. Once we grow adept at some aspect of this skill, generally one that comes more easily to us, we prefer to practice this element over and over. Our skill becomes lopsided as we avoid our weaknesses. Knowing that in our practice we can let down our guard, since we are not being watched or under pressure to perform, we bring to this a kind of dispersed attention. We tend to also be quite conventional in our practice routines. We generally follow what others have done, performing the accepted exercises for these skills.

This is the path of amateurs. To attain mastery, you must adopt what we shall call Resistance Practice. The principle is simple—you go in the opposite direction of all of your natural tendencies when it comes to practice. First, you *resist* the temptation to be nice to yourself. You become your own worst critic; you see your work as if through the eyes of others. You recognize your weaknesses, precisely the elements you are not good at. Those are the aspects you give precedence to in your practice. You find a kind of perverse pleasure in moving past the pain this might bring. Second, you *resist* the lure of easing up on your focus. You train yourself to concentrate in practice with double the intensity, as if it were the real thing times two. In devising your own routines, you become as creative as possible. You invent exercises that work upon your weaknesses. You give yourself arbitrary deadlines to meet certain standards, constantly pushing yourself past perceived limits. In this way you develop your own standards for excellence, generally higher than those of others.

In the end, your five hours of intense, focused work are the equivalent of ten for most people. Soon enough you will see the results of such practice, and others will marvel at the apparent ease in which you accomplish your deeds.

6. Apprentice yourself in failure

When it comes to being an entrepreneur, there is really only one effective form of apprenticeship—failure. It is like working on a machine: when a device malfunctions you do not take it personally or grow despondent. It is in fact a blessing in disguise. Such malfunctions generally show you inherent flaws and means of improvement. You simply keep tinkering until you get it right. The same should apply to your first entrepreneurial ventures. Mistakes and failures are precisely your means of education. They tell you about your own inadequacies. It is hard to find out such things from people, as they are often political with their praise and criticisms. Your failures also permit you to see the flaws of your ideas, which are only revealed in the execution of them. You learn what your audience or clients really want, the discrepancy between your ideas and how they affect the public.

Think of it this way: There are two kinds of failure. The first comes from never trying out your ideas because you are afraid, or because you are waiting for the perfect time. This kind of failure you can never learn from, and such timidity will destroy you. The second kind comes from a bold and venturesome spirit. If you fail in this way, the hit that you take to your reputation is greatly outweighed by what you learn. Repeated failure will toughen your spirit and show you with absolute clarity how things must be done. In fact, it is a curse to have everything go right on your first attempt. You will fail to question the element of luck, making you think that you have the golden touch. When you do inevitably fail, it will confuse and demoralize you past the point of learning. In any case, to apprentice as an entrepreneur you must act on your ideas as early as possible, exposing them to the public, a part of you even hoping that you'll fail. You have everything to gain.

7. Combine the "how" and the "what"

We humans live in two worlds. First, there is the outer world of appearances—all of the forms of things that captivate our eye. But hidden from our view is another world—how these things actually function, their anatomy or composition, the parts working together and forming the whole. This second world is not so immediately captivating. It is harder to understand. It is not something visible to the eye, but only to the mind that glimpses the reality. But this "how" of things is just as poetic once we understand it—it contains the secret of life, of how things move and change.

This division between the "how" and the "what" can be applied to almost everything around us—we see the machine, not how it works; we see a group of people producing something as a business, not how the group is structured or how the products are manufactured and distributed. (In a similar fashion, we tend to be mesmerized by people's appearances, not the psychology behind what they do or say.) In overcoming this division, in combining the "how" and the "what" of the field we work in, we gain a much deeper, or rather more rounded knowledge of it. We grasp a larger portion of the reality that goes into making whatever it is we produce.

Understand: we live in the world of a sad separation that began some five hundred years ago when art and science split apart. Scientists and technicians live in their own world, focusing mostly on the "how" of things. Others live in the world of appearances, using these things but not really understanding how they function. Just before this split occurred, it was the ideal of the Renaissance to combine these two forms of knowledge. This is why the work of Leonardo da Vinci continues to fascinate us, and why the Renaissance remains an ideal. This more rounded knowledge is in fact the way of the future, especially now that so much more information is available to all of us. This should be a part of our apprenticeship. We must make ourselves study as deeply as possible the technology we use, the functioning of the group we work in, the economics of our field, its lifeblood. We must constantly ask the questions—how do things work, how do decisions get made, how does the group interact? Rounding our knowledge in this way will give us a deeper feel for reality and the heightened power to alter it.

8. Advance through trial and error

Each age tends to create a model of apprenticeship that is suited to the system of production that prevails at the time. In the Middle Ages, during the birth of modern capitalism and the need for quality control, the first apprenticeship system appeared, with its rigidly defined terms. With the advent of the Industrial Revolution, this model of apprenticeship became largely outmoded, but the idea behind it lived on in the form of self-apprenticeship—developing yourself from within a particular field, as Darwin did in biology. This suited the growing individualistic spirit of the time. We are now in the information age, with computers dominating nearly all aspects of commercial life. Although there are many ways in which this could influence the concept of apprenticeship, it is the hacker approach to programming that may offer the most promising model for this new age.

The model goes like this: You want to learn as many skills as possible, following the direction that circumstances lead you to, but only if they are related to your deepest interests. Like a hacker, you value the process of self-discovery and making things that are of the highest quality. You avoid the trap of following one set career path. You are not sure where this will all lead, but you are taking full advantage of the openness of information, all of the knowledge about skills now at our disposal. You see what kind of work suits you and what you want to avoid at all cost. You move by trial and error. This is how you pass your twenties. You are the programmer of this wide-ranging apprenticeship, within the loose constraints of your personal interests.

You are not wandering about because you are afraid of commitment, but because you are expanding your skill base and your possibilities. At a certain point, when you are ready to settle on something, ideas and opportunities will inevitably present themselves to you. When that happens, all of the skills you have accumulated will prove invaluable. You will be the Master at combining them in ways that are unique and suited to your individuality. You may settle on this one place or idea for several years, accumulating in the process even more skills, then move in a slightly different direction when the time is appropriate. In this new age, those who follow a rigid, singular path in their youth often find themselves in a career dead end in their forties, or overwhelmed with boredom. The wide-ranging apprenticeship of your twenties will yield the opposite—expanding possibilities as you get older.

III

ABSORB THE MASTER'S POWER: THE MENTOR DYNAMIC

Life is short, and your time for learning and creativity is limited. Without any guidance, you can waste valuable years trying to gain knowledge and practice from various sources. Instead, you must follow the example set by Masters throughout the ages and find the proper mentor. The mentor-protégé relationship is the most efficient and productive form of learning. The right mentors know where to focus your attention and how to challenge you. Their knowledge and experience become yours. They provide immediate and realistic feedback on your work, so you can improve more rapidly. Choose the mentor who best fits your needs and connects to your Life's Task. Once you have internalized their knowledge, you must move on and never remain in their shadow. Your goal is always to surpass your mentors in mastery and brilliance.

THE ALCHEMY OF KNOWLEDGE

Growing up amid poverty in London, it seemed that the fate of Michael Faraday (1791–1867) was pretty much sealed for him at birth—he would either follow in his father's footsteps and become a blacksmith, or he would pursue some other manual trade. His options were severely limited by his circumstances. His parents had ten children to feed and support. The father worked sporadically because of illness, and the family needed additional income. The parents waited anxiously for the day when young Faraday would turn twelve and could get a job, or begin some kind of apprenticeship.

There was one trait, however, that marked him as different and was potentially troubling—he had an extremely active mind, one that was perhaps unsuited for a career that would entail mostly physical labor. When he was not doing errands and chores for his mother, he would wander the streets of central London, observing the world around him with utmost intensity. Nature, it seemed to him, was full of secrets that he wanted to ponder and unravel. Everything interested him, and his curiosity was limitless. He would ask endless questions of his parents, or anyone he could find, about plants or minerals or any seemingly inexplicable occurrence in nature. He seemed hungry for knowledge and frustrated by his lack of means to get it.

One day he wandered into a nearby shop that bound and sold books. The sight of so many shiny books on the shelves astounded him. His own schooling had been minimal, and he had really only known one book in his life, the Bible. To Faraday, who came from a very religious family, the printed words of the Bible had a kind of magical power. He imagined that each of the books in this shop opened up different worlds of knowledge, a form of magic in its own right.

The owner of the shop, George Riebau, was instantly charmed by the young man's reverence for his books. He had never met someone quite so intense at such a young age. He encouraged him to return, and soon Faraday began to frequent the shop. To help Faraday's family, Riebau gave him a job as a delivery boy. Impressed with his work ethic, he invited him to join the shop itself as an apprentice bookbinder. Faraday happily accepted, and in 1805 he began his seven-year apprenticeship.

In the initial months of the job, surrounded by all these books, the young man could hardly believe his good fortune—new books were rare commodities in those days, luxury items for the well-to-do. Not even a public library contained what could be found in Riebau's shop. The owner encouraged him to read whatever he liked in his off-hours, and Faraday obliged by devouring almost every single book that passed through his hands. One evening he read an encyclopedia passage on the most recent discoveries in electricity, and he suddenly felt as if he had found his calling in life. Here was a phenomenon that was invisible to the eye, but that could be revealed and measured through experiments. This process of uncovering nature's secrets through experiment enthralled him. Science, it seemed to him, was a great quest to unravel the mysteries of Creation itself. Somehow, he would transform himself into a scientist.

This was not a realistic goal on his part and he knew it. In England at the time, access to laboratories and to science as a career was only open to those with a university education, which meant those from the upper classes. How could a bookbinder's apprentice even dream of overcoming such odds? Even if he had the energy and desire to attempt it, he had no teachers, no guidance, no structure or method to his studies. Then in 1809 a book came into the shop that finally gave him some hope. It was called *Improvement of the Mind*—a self-help guide written by Reverend Isaac Watts, first published in 1741. The book revealed a system of learning and improving your lot in life, no matter your social class. It prescribed courses of action that anyone could follow, and it promised results. Faraday read it over and over, carrying it with him wherever he went.

He followed the book's advice to the letter. For Watts, learning had to be an active process. He recommended not just reading about scientific discoveries, but actually re-creating the experiments that led to them. And so, with Riebau's blessing, Faraday began a series of basic experiments in electricity and chemistry in the back room of the shop. Watts advocated the importance of having teachers and not just learning from books. Faraday dutifully began to attend the numerous lectures on science that were popular in London at the time.

Watts advocated not just listening to lectures but taking detailed notes, then reworking the notes themselves—all of this imprinting the knowledge deeper in the brain. Faraday would take this even further.

Attending the lectures of the popular scientist John Tatum, each week on a different subject, he would note down the most important words and concepts, quickly sketch out the various instruments Tatum used, and diagram the experiments. Over the next few days he would expand the notes into sentences, and then into an entire chapter on the subject, elaborately sketched and narrated. In the course of a year this added up to a thick scientific encyclopedia he had created on his own. His knowledge of science had grown by leaps and bounds, and had assumed a kind of organizational shape modeled on his notes.

One day, Monsieur Riebau showed this rather impressive collection of notes to a customer named William Dance, a member of the prestigious Royal Institution, an organization that sought to promote the latest advances in science. Thumbing through Faraday's chapters, Dance was astounded at how clearly and concisely he had summarized complicated topics. He decided to invite the young man to attend a series of lectures by the renowned and recently knighted chemist Humphry Davy, to be given at the Royal Institution where Davy was director of the chemistry laboratory.

The lectures had been sold out well in advance and this was a rare privilege for a young man of Faraday's background, but for him it was much more fateful than that. Davy was the preeminent chemist of his time; he had made numerous discoveries and was advancing the new field of electrochemistry. His experiments with various gases and chemicals were highly dangerous and had led to numerous accidents. This only added to his reputation as a fearless warrior for science. His lectures were events—he had a flair for the dramatic, performing clever experiments before a dazzled audience. He came from a modest background and had raised himself to the heights of science, having gained the attention of some valuable mentors. To Faraday, Davy was the only living scientist he could model himself after, considering Davy's lack of any solid formal education.

Arriving early each time and gaining the closest seat he could find, he soaked up every aspect of Davy's lectures, taking the most detailed notes he had ever attempted. These lectures had a different effect upon Faraday than others he had attended. He was inspired and yet he also could not help but feel somewhat dejected. After all of these years of studying on his own, he had managed to expand his knowledge of science and of the natural world. But science does not consist of the accumulation of information. It is a way of thinking, of approaching problems. The scientific spirit is creative—Faraday could feel it in Davy's presence. As an amateur scientist looking at the field from the outside, his knowledge was one-dimensional and would lead nowhere. He needed to move to the inside, where he could gain practical, hands-on experience, become part of the community and learn how to think like a scientist. And to move closer to this scientific spirit and absorb its essence, he would need a mentor.

This seemed like an impossible quest, but with his apprenticeship coming to an end, and facing the prospect of being a bookbinder for life, Faraday went into desperation mode. He wrote letters to the president of the Royal Society and applied for the most menial jobs in any kind of laboratory. He was relentless, and yet months went by with no results. Then one day, out of the blue, he received a message from Humphry Davy's office. The chemist had been blinded by yet another explosion in his laboratory at the Royal Institution, and the condition would last for several days. During this time he needed a personal assistant to take notes and organize his materials. Mr. Dance, a good friend of Davy's, had recommended young Faraday for the job.

There seemed something fateful, even magical, in this occurrence. Faraday would have to make the most of it, do whatever he could to impress the great chemist. Awestruck to be in Davy's presence, Faraday listened with utmost intensity to every one of his instructions and did more than was asked for. When Davy, however, had recovered his sight, he thanked Faraday for his work but made it clear that the Royal Institution already had a laboratory assistant and there were simply no openings for him on any level.

Faraday felt despondent, but he was not ready to give up; he would not let this be the end. Only a few days in Davy's presence had revealed so many learning possibilities. Davy liked to talk about his ideas as they occurred to him and gain feedback from anyone around him. Discussing with Faraday one experiment he was planning afforded the young man a glimpse into how his mind worked, and it was fascinating. Davy would be the ultimate mentor, and Faraday determined that he would have to make this happen. He went back to the notes he had taken on Davy's lectures. He worked them into a beautifully organized booklet, carefully handwritten, and full of sketches and diagrams. He sent this off to Davy as a gift. He then wrote to him a few weeks later, reminding Davy about the experiment he had mentioned but had probably forgotten about—Davy was notoriously absentminded. Faraday heard nothing. But then one day, in February 1813, he was suddenly summoned to the Royal Institution.

That same morning the Institution's laboratory assistant had been fired for insubordination. They needed to replace him immediately, and Davy had recommended young Faraday. The job mostly involved cleaning bottles and equipment, sweeping, and lighting fireplaces. The pay was low, considerably lower than what he could gain as a bookbinder, but Faraday, hardly believing his good fortune, accepted on the spot.

His education was so rapid it shocked him; it was nothing like the progress he had made on his own. Under his mentor's supervision, he learned how to prepare Davy's chemical mixtures, including some of the more explosive varieties. He was taught the rudiments of chemical analysis from perhaps the greatest living practitioner of the art. His responsibilities began to grow, and he was given access to the lab for his own experiments. He worked night and day to bring a much-needed order to the laboratory and its shelves. He watched Davy closely at work, taking careful note of his highly creative way of devising crucial experiments that physically demonstrated his ideas. And slowly, their relationship deepened—clearly Davy saw him as a younger version of himself.

By the year 1821, however, Faraday had to confront an unpleasant reality: Davy was keeping him under his thumb. After eight years of an intense apprenticeship, he was now an accomplished chemist in his own right, with expanding knowledge of other sciences. He was doing independent research, but Davy was still treating him as an assistant, making him send packets of dead flies for his fishing lures and assigning him other menial tasks.

It was Davy who had rescued him from the drudgery of the bookbinding business. He owed him everything. But Faraday was now thirty years old, and if he were not allowed soon enough to declare his independence, his most creative years would be wasted as a laboratory assistant. To leave on bad terms, however, would ruin his name in the scientific community, especially considering his own lack of reputation. Then, finally, Faraday found a chance to separate himself from his overbearing mentor, and he exploited this opportunity to the maximum.

Scientists throughout Europe were making discoveries about the relationship between electricity and magnetism, but the effect they had on each other was strange—creating a movement that was not linear and direct, but apparently more circular. Nothing in nature was quite like this. How to reveal the exact shape of this effect or movement in an experiment became the rage, and soon Davy got involved. Working with a fellow scientist named William Hyde Wollaston, they proposed the idea that the movement created by electromagnetism was more like a spiral. Involving Faraday in their experiments, they devised a way to break up the movement into small increments that could be measured. Once this was all added up, it would show the spiral motion.

At about the same time, Faraday was asked by a close friend to write a review of all that was known about electromagnetism for an established journal, and so he began a rigorous study of the field. Thinking like his mentor, he speculated that there must be a way to physically demonstrate the motion created by electromagnetism in a continual fashion, so that no one could dispute the results. One night in September 1821 he had a vision of just such an experiment, and he put it into practice. With a bar magnet secured upright in a cup of liquid mercury (a metal that conducts electricity), Faraday placed a suspended wire, buoyed by a cork, in the mercury. When the wire was charged with electricity, the cork moved around the magnet in a precise conical path. The reverse experiment (with the wire secured in the water) revealed the same pattern.

This was the first time in history that electricity had

been used to generate continual motion, the precursor to all electric motors. The experiment was so simple and yet only Faraday had seen it so clearly. It revealed a way of thinking that was very much the product of Davy's tutelage. Excited about what he had done, he rushed to have his results published.

In his haste to get his report out, however, Faraday had forgotten to mention the research done by Wollaston and Davy. Soon enough, the rumor spread that Faraday had actually plagiarized their work. Realizing his mistake, Faraday met with Wollaston and showed him how he had reached his results independent of anyone else's work. Wollaston agreed and let the matter drop. But the rumors continued, and soon it became clear that the source of them was Davy himself. He refused to accept Faraday's explanation and no one knew quite why. When Faraday was nominated to the Royal Society because of his discovery, it was Davy, as president, who tried to block it. A year later, when Faraday made yet another important discovery, Davy claimed partial credit for it. He seemed to believe that he had created Faraday from nothing and so was responsible for everything he did.

Faraday had seen enough—their relationship was essentially over. He would never correspond with or see him again. Now having authority within the scientific community, Faraday could do as he pleased. His coming experiments would soon pave the way for all of the most important advances in electrical energy, and for the field theories that would revolutionize science in the twentieth century. He would go on to become one of history's greatest practitioners of experimental science, far outshining the fame of his one-time mentor.

KEYS TO MASTERY

In the past, people of power had an aura of authority that was very real. Some of this aura emanated from their accomplishments, and some of it from the position they occupied—being a member of the aristocracy or a religious elite. This aura had a definite effect and could be felt; it caused people to respect and worship those who possessed it. Over the centuries, however, the slow process of democratization has worn away this aura of authority in all of its guises, to the point today of almost nonexistence.

We feel, rightly so, that no one should be admired or worshipped merely for the position they occupy, particularly if it comes from connections or a privileged background. But this attitude carries over to people who have reached their position mostly through their own accomplishments. We live in a culture that likes to criticize and debunk any form of authority, to point out the weaknesses of those in power. If we feel any aura, it is in the presence of celebrities and their seductive personalities. Some of this skeptical spirit toward authority is healthy, particularly in relation to politics, but when it comes to learning and the Apprenticeship Phase, it presents a problem.

To learn requires a sense of humility. We must admit that there are people out there who know our field much more deeply than we do. Their superiority is not a function of natural talent or privilege, but rather of time and experience. But if we are not comfortable with this fact, if we feel in general mistrustful of any kind of authority, we will succumb to the belief that we can just as easily learn something on our own, that being self-taught is more authentic. We feel, perhaps unconsciously, that learning from Masters and submitting to their authority is somehow an indictment of our own natural ability. Even if we have teachers in our lives, we tend not to pay full attention to their advice, often preferring to do things our own way.

Understand: all that should concern you in the early stages of your career is acquiring practical knowledge in the most efficient manner possible. For this purpose, during the Apprenticeship Phase you will need mentors whose authority you recognize and to whom you submit. Your admission of need does not say anything essential about you, but only about your temporary condition of weakness, which your mentor will help you overcome.

The reason you require a mentor is simple: Life is short; you have only so much time and so much energy to expend. You can learn what you need through books, your own practice, and occasional advice from others, but the process is hit-and-miss. The information in books is not tailored to your circumstances and individuality; it tends to be somewhat abstract and hard to put into practice. You can learn from your experiences, but it can often take years to fully understand the meaning of what has happened. It is always possible to practice on your own, but you will not receive enough focused feedback. You can often gain a self-directed apprenticeship in many fields, but this could take ten years, maybe more.

Mentors do not give you a shortcut, but they streamline the process. They invariably had their own great mentors, giving them a richer and deeper knowledge of their field. Their ensuing years of experience taught them invaluable lessons and strategies for learning. Their knowledge and experience become yours; they can direct you away from unnecessary side paths or errors. They observe you at work and provide real-time feedback, making your practice more time efficient. Working closely with them, you absorb the essence of their creative spirit, which you can now adapt in your own way. What took you ten years on your own could have been done in five with proper direction.

What makes the mentor-protégé dynamic so intense and so productive is the emotional quality of the relationship. By nature, mentors feel emotionally invested in your education. On your part, you also feel emotionally drawn to them—admiration for their achievements, a desire to model yourself after them, and so on. Mentors find this immensely flattering.

With this two-way emotional connection you both open up to each other in a way that goes beyond the usual teacher-student dynamic.

Think of it this way: the process of learning

resembles the medieval practice of alchemy. In alchemy, the goal was to find a way to transform base metals or stones into gold. To effect this, alchemists searched for what was known as the philosopher's stone—a substance that would make dead stones or metals come alive and organically change their chemical composition into gold. Although the philosopher's stone was never discovered, it has profound relevance as a metaphor. The knowledge that you need to become a Master exists out there in the world—it is like a base metal or dead stone. This knowledge needs to be heated up and come alive within you, transforming itself into something active and relevant to your circumstances. The mentor is like the philosopher's stone—through direct interaction with someone of experience, you are able to quickly and efficiently heat up and animate this knowledge, turning it into something like gold.

To initially entice the right Master to serve as your mentor, you will want to mix in a strong element of self-interest. You have something tangible and practical to offer them, in addition to your youth and energy. Before he had ever met him, Davy was aware of Faraday's work ethic and organizational skills. That alone made him a desirable assistant. Considering this, you may not want to go in search of mentors until you have acquired some elementary skills and discipline that you can rely upon to interest them.

Almost all Masters and people of power suffer from too many demands on their time and too much information to absorb. If you can demonstrate the ability to help them organize themselves on these fronts to a degree that others cannot, it will be much easier to get their attention and interest them in the relationship.

You will want as much personal interaction with the mentor as possible. A virtual relationship is never enough. There are cues and subtle aspects you can only pick up through a person-to-person interaction—such as a way of doing things that has evolved through much experience. It was only through constant exposure to Davy's thought process that Faraday understood the power of finding the crucial experiment to demonstrate an idea, something he would adapt later on with great success.

Mentors have their own strengths and weaknesses. The good ones allow you to develop your own style and then to leave them when the time is right. Such types can remain lifelong friends and allies. But often the opposite will occur. They grow dependent on your services and want to keep you indentured. They envy your youth and unconsciously hinder you, or become overcritical. You must be aware of this as it develops. Your goal is to get as much out of them as possible, but at a certain point you may pay a price if you stay too long and let them subvert your confidence. Your submitting to their authority is by no means unconditional, and in fact your goal all along is eventually to find your way to independence, having internalized and adapted their wisdom.

You must not allow yourself to feel any guilt when the time comes to assert yourself. Instead, as Faraday did, you should feel resentful and even angry about his desire to hold you back, using such emotions to help you leave him.

In any event, you will probably have several mentors in your life, like stepping-stones along the way to mastery. At each phase of life you must find the appropriate teachers, getting what you want out of them, moving on, and feeling no shame for this. It is the path your own mentor probably took and it is the way of the world.

STRATEGIES FOR DEEPENING THE MENTOR DYNAMIC

One repays a teacher badly if one remains only a pupil.

—FRIEDRICH NIETZSCHE

Although you must submit to the authority of mentors in order to learn from and absorb their power to the highest degree, this does not mean you remain passive in the process. At certain critical points, you can set and determine the dynamic, personalize it to suit your purposes. The following four strategies are designed to help you exploit the relationship to the fullest and transform the knowledge you gain into creative energy.

1. Choose the mentor according to your needs and inclinations

The choice of the right mentor is more important than you might imagine. Because so much of his or her future influence upon you can be deeper than you are consciously aware of, the wrong choice can have a net negative effect upon your journey to mastery. You could end up absorbing conventions and styles that don't fit you and that will confuse you later on. If he or she is too domineering, you could end up becoming a lifelong imitation of the mentor, instead of a Master in your own right. People often err in this process when they choose someone who seems the most knowledgeable, has a charming personality, or has the most stature in the field—all superficial reasons. Do not simply choose the first possible mentor who crosses your path. Be prepared to put as much thought into it as possible.

In selecting a mentor, you will want to keep in mind your inclinations and Life's Task, the future position you envision for yourself. The mentor you choose should be strategically aligned with this. If your path is in a more revolutionary direction, you will want a mentor who is open, progressive, and not domineering. If your ideal aligns more with a style that is somewhat idiosyncratic, you will want a mentor who will make you feel comfortable with this and help you transform your peculiarities into mastery, instead of trying to squelch them. If you are somewhat confused and ambivalent about your direction, it can be useful to choose someone who can help you gain some clarity about what you want, someone important in the field who might not fit perfectly with your tastes. Sometimes part of what a mentor shows us is something we will want to avoid or actively rebel against. In this latter case, you might initially want to maintain a little more emotional distance than normally recommended, particularly if he or she is the domineering type. Over time you will see what to absorb and what to reject.

The Mentor Dynamic replays something of the parental or father-figure dynamic. It is a cliché that you do not get to choose the family you are born into, but you are happily free to choose your mentors. In this case, the right choice can perhaps provide what your parents didn't give you—support, confidence, direction, space to discover things on your own. Look for mentors who can do that, and beware of falling into the opposite trap—opting for a mentor who resembles one of your parents, including all of his or her negative traits. You will merely repeat what hampered you in the first place.

2. Gaze deep into the mentor's mirror

To reach mastery requires some toughness and a constant connection to reality. As an apprentice, it can be hard for us to challenge ourselves on our own in the proper way, and to get a clear sense of our own weaknesses. The times that we live in make this even harder. Developing discipline through challenging situations and perhaps suffering along the way are no longer values that are promoted in our culture. People are increasingly reluctant to tell each other the truth about themselves—their weaknesses, their inadequacies, flaws in their work. Even the self-help books designed to set us straight tend to be soft and flattering, telling us what we want to hear—that we are basically good and can get what we want by following a few simple steps. It seems abusive or damaging to people's self-esteem to offer them stern, realistic criticism, to set them tasks that will make them aware of how far they have to go. In fact, this indulgence and fear of hurting people's feelings is far more abusive in the long run. It makes it hard for people to gauge where they are or to develop self-discipline. It makes them unsuited for the rigors of the journey to mastery. It weakens people's will.

Masters are those who by nature have suffered to get to where they are. They have experienced endless criticisms of their work, doubts about their progress, set-backs along the way. They know deep in their bones what is required to get to the creative phase and beyond. As mentors, they alone can gauge the extent of our progress, the weaknesses in our character, the ordeals we must go through to advance. In this day and age, you must get the sharpest dose of reality that is possible from your mentor. You must go in search of it and welcome it. If possible, choose a mentor who is known for supplying this form of tough love. If they shy away from giving it, force them to hold up the mirror that will reflect you as you are. Get them to give you the proper challenges that will reveal your strengths and weaknesses and allow you to gain as much feedback as possible, no matter how hard it might be to take. Accustom yourself to criticism. Confidence is important, but if it is not based on a realistic appraisal of who you are, it is mere grandiosity and smugness. Through the realistic feedback of your mentor you will eventually develop a confidence that is much more substantial and worth possessing.

3. Transfigure their ideas

As apprentices, we all face the following dilemma: To learn from mentors, we must be open and completely receptive to their ideas. We must fall under their spell. But if we take this too far, we become so marked by their influence that we have no internal space to incubate and develop our own voice, and we spend our lives tied to ideas that are not our own. The solution is simple yet subtle: Even as we listen and incorporate the ideas of our mentors, we must slowly cultivate some distance from them. We begin by gently adapting their ideas to our circumstances, altering them to fit our style and inclinations. As we progress we can become bolder, even focusing on faults or weaknesses in some of their ideas. We slowly mold their knowledge into our own shape. As we grow in confidence and contemplate our independence, we can even grow competitive with the mentor we once worshipped. Establishing our differences with the mentor is an important part of our self-development. As Leonardo da Vinci said, "Poor is the apprentice who does not surpass his Master."

4. Create a back-and-forth dynamic

In theory, there should be no limit to what we can learn from mentors who have wide experience. But in practice, this is rarely the case. The reasons are several: at some point the relationship can become flat; it is difficult for us to maintain the same level of attention that we had in the beginning. We might come to resent their authority a little, especially as we gain in skill and the difference between us becomes somewhat less. Also, they come from a different generation, with a different worldview. At a certain point, some of their cherished principles might seem a bit out of touch or irrelevant, and we unconsciously tune them out. The only solution is to evolve a more interactive dynamic with the mentor. If they can adapt to some of your ideas, the relationship becomes more animated. Feeling a growing openness on their part to your input, you are less resentful. You are revealing to them your own experiences and ideas, perhaps loosening them up so their principles don't harden into dogma.

Such a style of interaction is more in tune with our democratic times and can serve as something of an ideal. But it should not go along with a rebellious attitude or a lessening in respect. The dynamic sketched out earlier in this chapter remains the same. You bring to the relationship the utmost in admiration and your total attention. You are completely open to their instruction. Gaining their respect for how teachable you are, they will fall a bit under your spell. With your intense focus, you improve in your skill levels, giving you the power to introduce more of yourself and your needs. You give them feedback to their instruction, perhaps adjust some of their ideas. This must begin with you, as you set the tone with your hunger to learn. Once a back-and-forth dynamic is sparked, the relationship has almost limitless potential for learning and absorbing power.

IV

SEE PEOPLE AS THEY ARE: SOCIAL INTELLIGENCE

Often the greatest obstacle to our pursuit of mastery comes from the emotional drain we experience in dealing with the resistance and manipulations of the people around us. The principal problem we face in the social arena is our naïve tendency to project onto people our emotional needs and desires of the moment. Social intelligence is the ability to see people in the most realistic light possible. By moving past our usual self-absorption, we can learn to focus deeply on others, reading their behavior in the moment, seeing what motivates them, and discerning any possible manipulative tendencies. Success attained without this intelligence is not true mastery, and will not last.

THINKING INSIDE

In 1718, Benjamin Franklin (1706–90) went to work as an apprentice in his brother James's printing shop in Boston. His dream was to transform himself into a great writer. At the printing shop he would not only be taught how to handle the machines, but also how to edit manuscripts. Surrounded by books and newspapers, he would have plenty of examples of good writing to study and learn from.

As the apprenticeship progressed, the literary education he had imagined for himself came to pass, and his writing skills improved immensely. Then, in 1722, it seemed that he would finally have the perfect opportunity to prove himself as a writer—his brother was about to launch his own large-scale newspaper called *The New-England Courant*. Benjamin approached James with several interesting ideas for stories he could write, but to his great disappointment, his brother was not interested in his contributing to the new paper.

Benjamin knew it was pointless to argue with James; he was a very stubborn young man. But as he thought about the situation, an idea suddenly came to him: what if he were to create a fictional character who would write letters to *The Courant*? If he wrote them well enough, James would never suspect they were from Benjamin, and he would print them. After much thinking, he decided upon the perfect character to create: a young female widow named Silence Dogood who had lots of strong opinions about life in Boston, many of them quite absurd.

He sent the first, rather lengthy letter to *The Courant* and watched with amusement as his brother published it and added a note in the newspaper asking for more letters from her. James continued publishing the subsequent letters, and they quickly became the most popular part of *The Courant*.

Benjamin's responsibilities at the shop began to grow, and he proved to be quite an adept editor for the newspaper as well. Feeling proud of all his precocious achievements, one day he could not help himself—he confessed to James that he was the author of the Dogood letters. Expecting some praise for this, he was surprised by James's vitriolic response—his brother did not like being lied to. To make matters worse, over the next few months he turned increasingly cold and even abusive to Benjamin. It soon became impossible to work for him, and by the fall of 1723, Benjamin decided to flee Boston, turning his back on brother and family.

After several weeks of wandering he ended up in Philadelphia, determined to settle there. He was only seventeen, with virtually no money and no contacts, but for some reason he felt full of hope. In the five years working for his brother he had learned more about the business than men twice his age. Sure enough, within a few weeks he managed to secure a position at one of the two printing shops in town, owned by a man named Samuel Keimer. Philadelphia was still relatively small and provincial at the time—word spread quickly of the newcomer and his literary skills.

The governor of the colony of Pennsylvania,

William Keith, had ambitions of transforming Philadelphia into a cultural center, and was not happy with the two established printing businesses. Hearing of Benjamin Franklin and of his writing talent, he sought him out. Clearly impressed with the young man's intelligence, he urged him to start his own printing shop, promising to lend him the initial amount that was needed to get the business going. The machines and materials would have to come from London, and Keith advised him to go there personally to supervise the acquisition. He had contacts there and would bankroll it all.

Franklin could hardly believe his good fortune. As he made his plans for London, the money Keith had promised as a loan was not forthcoming, but after writing to him a few times, word finally came from the governor's office not to worry—letters of credit would be waiting for him once he disembarked in England. And so, without explaining to Keimer what he was up to, he quit his job and bought his passage for the transatlantic journey.

When he got to England there were no letters waiting. Feeling there must have been some kind of miscommunication, he frantically looked in London for a representative of the governor to whom he could explain their agreement. In his search he came upon a wealthy merchant from Philadelphia who, hearing his story, revealed to him the truth—Governor Keith was a notorious talker. He was always promising everything to everyone, trying to impress people with his power. His enthusiasm for a scheme would rarely last more than a week. He had no money to lend, and his character was worth about as much as his promises.

As Franklin took this all in and considered his current predicament, what disturbed him was not that he now found himself in a precarious position—alone and without money, far from home. There was no place more exciting for a young man than London, and he would somehow make his way there. What bothered him was how badly he had misread Keith and how naïve he had been.

Fortunately, London was teeming with large-scale printing shops, and within a few weeks of his arrival he found a position within one of them. He got along well enough with his colleagues, but soon he encountered a strange British custom: five times a day his fellow printers would take a break to drink a pint of beer. It fortified them for the work, or so they said. Every week Franklin was expected to contribute to the beer fund for those in the room, including himself, but he refused to pay up—he did not like to drink during working hours, and the idea that he should give up a part of his hard-earned wages for others to ruin their health made him angry. He spoke honestly about his principles, and they politely accepted his decision.

Over the ensuing weeks, however, strange things began to happen: mistakes kept popping up in texts he had already proofread, and almost every day he noticed some new error for which he was blamed. Clearly, somebody was sabotaging his work, and when he complained to his fellow printers, they attributed it all to a mischievous ghost who was known to haunt the room. Finally figuring out what this meant, he let go of his principles and contributed to the beer fund; the mistakes suddenly disappearing along with the ghost.

After this incident and several other indiscretions in London, Franklin began to seriously wonder about himself. He seemed hopelessly naïve, constantly misreading the intentions of the people around him. Thinking about this problem, he was struck by an apparent paradox: when it came to his work, he was supremely rational and realistic, always looking to improve himself. But with people it was virtually the opposite: he would inevitably become swept up in his emotions and lose all contact with reality. With his brother, he wanted to impress him by revealing his authorship of the letters, totally unaware of the envy and malevolence he would unleash; with Keith, he was so wrapped up in his dreams that he paid no attention to obvious signs that the governor was all talk; with the printers, his anger blinded him to the fact that they would obviously resent his attempts at reform.

Determined to break this pattern and change his ways, he decided there was only one solution: in all of his future interactions with people, he would force himself to take an initial step backward and not get emotional. From this more detached position, he would focus completely on the people he was dealing with, cutting off his own insecurities and desires from the equation. Gaining position inside people's minds, he could see how to melt their resistance or thwart their malevolent plans.

After more than a year and a half of work in London, Franklin finally saved enough money for his return journey to the colonies, and in 1727 he found himself back in Philadelphia, looking once more for work. In the midst of his search, his former employer, Samuel Keimer, surprised him by offering Franklin a nice position in the printing shop—he would be in charge of the staff and training the others Keimer had recently hired as part of his expanding business. For this he would receive a nice yearly salary. Franklin accepted, but almost from the beginning he could sense something was not right. And so, as he had promised himself, he took a step back and calmly reviewed the facts.

He had five men to train, but once he accomplished this task there would be little work left over for him. Keimer himself had been acting strangely—much friendlier than usual. He was an insecure and prickly gentleman, and this friendly front did not fit him. Imagining the situation from Keimer's perspective, he could sense that he must have greatly resented Franklin's sudden departure for London, leaving him in the lurch. He must have seen Franklin as a young whippersnapper who needed his comeuppance. He was not the type to discuss this with anyone, but would seethe from within and scheme on his own. Thinking in this way, Keimer's intentions became clear to him: he was planning to get Franklin to impart his extensive knowledge of the business to the new employees, then fire him. This would be his revenge.

Certain he had read this correctly, he decided to

quietly turn the tables. He used his new managerial position to build relationships with customers and to connect with successful merchants in the area. He experimented with some new manufacturing methods he had learned in England. When Keimer was away from the shop, he taught himself new skills such as engraving and ink-making. He paid close attention to his pupils, and carefully cultivated one of them to be a first-rate assistant. And just when he suspected that Keimer was about to fire him, he left and set up his own shop—with financial backing, greater knowledge of the business, a solid base of customers who would follow him everywhere, and a first-rate assistant whom he had trained. In executing this strategy, Franklin noticed how free he was from any feelings of bitterness or anger toward Keimer. It was all maneuvers on a chessboard, and by thinking inside Keimer he was able to play the game to perfection, with a clear and level head.

Over the ensuing years, Franklin's printing business prospered. He became an increasingly prominent member of the Philadelphia community, even entering into politics. He was thought of as the quintessence of the trustworthy merchant and citizen. Like his fellow townsfolk, he dressed plainly; he worked harder than anyone they knew; he never frequented bars or gambling houses; and he had a folksy and even humble manner. His popularity was almost universal. But in the last public chapter of his life, he acted in a way that seemed to indicate that he had changed and lost his common touch.

In 1776, a year after the outbreak of the War of Independence, Franklin—now a distinguished political figure in America—was dispatched to France as a special commissioner to obtain arms, financing and an alliance. Soon stories spread throughout the colonies of his various intrigues with French women and courtesans, and of his attendance at lavish parties and dinners—much of which was true. Prominent politicians such as John Adams accused him of becoming corrupted by the Parisians. His popularity among Americans plummeted. But what the critics and public did not realize was that wherever he went he assumed the look, the outward morals, and the behavior of the culture at hand, so that he could better make his way. Desperate to win the French over to the American cause and understanding their nature quite well, he had transformed himself into what they had wanted to see in him—the American version of the French spirit and way of life. He was appealing to their notorious narcissism.

All of this worked to perfection—Franklin became a beloved figure to the French, and a man of influence with their government. In the end, he brokered an important military alliance and gained the kind of financing nobody else could have wrested from the stingy French king. This final public act in his life was not an aberration, but the ultimate application of his social rationality.

KEYS TO MASTERY

We humans are the preeminent social animal. In theory, all of us today possess the natural tools—empathy, rational thinking—to have a supreme understanding of our fellow humans. In practice, however, these tools remain mostly undeveloped, and the explanation for this can be found in the peculiar nature of our childhood, and our extended period of dependency.

During this time of weakness and dependency, we experience the need to idealize our parents. Our survival depends on their strength and reliability. To think of them as having their own frailties would fill us with unbearable anxiety. And so we inevitably see them as stronger, more capable, and more selfless than they are in reality.

Then inevitably, often in adolescence, we start to glimpse a less-than-noble side to many people, including our parents, and we cannot help but feel upset at the disparity between what we had imagined and the reality. In our disappointment, we tend to exaggerate their negative qualities, much as we once had exaggerated the positive ones.

Let us call this the *Naïve Perspective*. Although it is natural to have such a perspective because of the unique character of our childhood, it is also dangerous because it envelops us in childish illusions about people, distorting our view of them. We carry this perspective with us into the adult world, into the Apprenticeship Phase. In the work environment the stakes are suddenly raised.

People reveal qualities of their characters that they normally try to conceal. They manipulate, compete, and think of themselves first. We are blindsided by this behavior and our emotions are churned up even more than before, locking us into the Naïve Perspective.

This perspective makes us feel sensitive and vulnerable. Looking inward as to how the words and actions of others implicate us in some way, we continually misread their intentions. We project our own feelings onto them. We have no real sense of what they are thinking or what motivates them. With the inevitable mistakes we make, we become entangled in battles and dramas that consume our minds and distract us from learning. Our sense of priorities becomes warped—we end up giving far too much importance to social and political issues because we are not handling them well.

Social intelligence is nothing more than the process of discarding the Naïve Perspective and approaching something more realistic. It involves focusing our attention outward instead of inward, honing the observational and empathic skills that we naturally possess. It means moving past our tendency to idealize and demonize people, and seeing and accepting them as they are.

Following Benjamin Franklin's example, you can reach this awareness by reviewing your past, paying particular attention to any battles, mistakes, tensions, or disappointments on the social front. If you look at these events through the lens of the Naïve Perspective, you will focus only on what *other people* have done to you—the mistreatments you endured from them, the slights or injuries you felt. Instead, you must turn this around and begin with yourself—how *you* saw in others qualities they did not possess, or how *you* ignored signs of a dark side to their nature.

This new clarity about your perspective should be accompanied by an adjustment of your attitude. The world is full of people with different characters and temperaments. You cannot change people at their core, but must merely avoid becoming their victim. You are an observer of the human comedy, and by being as tolerant as possible, you gain a much greater ability to understand people and to influence their behavior when necessary.

With this new awareness and attitude in place, you can begin to advance in your apprenticeship in social intelligence. This intelligence consists of two components, both equally important to master. First, there is what we shall call *specific knowledge of human nature*— namely the ability to read people, to get a feel for how they see the world, and to understand their individuality. Second, there is the *general knowledge of human nature*, which means accumulating an understanding of the overall patterns of human behavior that transcend us as individuals, including some of the darker qualities we often disregard. Only the possession of both forms of knowledge can give you a complete picture of the people around you.

Specific Knowledge—Reading People

Most of us have had the sensation at some point in our lives of experiencing an uncanny connection with another person. In such moments we have an understanding that is hard to put into words; we even feel that we can anticipate the thoughts of the other person. Such communication generally occurs with close friends and partners, people whom we trust and feel attuned to on many levels. In these moments of connection, the internal monologue is shut off, and we pick up more cues and signals from the other person than usual.

What this means is that when we are not inward-directed but attending more deeply to another person, we gain access to forms of communication that are largely nonverbal in nature, and quite effective in their own way.

The intense nonverbal connection we experience with those we are close to is clearly not appropriate in a work environment, but to the degree we open ourselves up and direct our attention outward to other people, we can become much more effective at reading people.

To begin this process, you need to train yourself to pay less attention to the words that people say and greater attention to their tone of voice, the look in their eye, their body language—all signals that might reveal a nervousness or excitement that is not expressed verbally. If you can get people to become emotional, they will reveal a lot more.

On this nonverbal level, it is interesting to observe

how people behave around those in positions of power and authority. They will tend to reveal an anxiety, a resentment, or a sycophantic falseness that betrays something essential about their psychological makeup, something that goes back to their childhoods and that can be read in their body language.

As an exercise, after you have known people for a while, try to imagine that you are experiencing the world from their point of view, placing yourself in their circumstances and feeling what they feel. Look for any common emotional experiences—a trauma or difficulty you've had, for instance, that resembles in some way what they are going through. Reliving a part of that emotion can help you begin the identifying process.

This intuitive form of reading people becomes more effective and accurate the more you use it, but it is best to combine it with other, more conscious forms of observation. For instance, you should take particular note of people's actions and decisions. Your goal is to figure out the hidden motives behind them, which will often revolve around power. People will say all kinds of things about their motives and intentions; they are used to dressing things up with words. Their actions, however, say much more about their character, about what is going on underneath the surface.

You should be sensitive to any kind of extreme behavior on their part—for instance, a blustery front, an overly friendly manner, a constant penchant for jokes. You will often notice that they wear this like a mask to hide the opposite, to distract others from the truth. They are blustery because they are inwardly very insecure; they are overly friendly because they are secretly ambitious and aggressive; or they joke to hide a mean-spiritedness.

In general, you are reading and decoding every possible sign—including the clothes they wear and the organized or disorganized nature of their workspace. The choice of mate or partner can be quite eloquent too, particularly if it seems slightly inconsistent with the character they try to project. In this choice they can reveal unmet needs from childhood, a desire for power and control, a low self-image, and other qualities they normally seek to disguise. What might seem like small issues—chronically being late, insufficient attention to detail, not returning any favors on your part—are signs of something deeper about their character. These are patterns you must pay attention to. Nothing is too small to notice.

General Knowledge—The Seven Deadly Realities

Throughout recorded history we can detect patterns of human behavior that transcend culture and time, indicating certain universal features that belong to us as a species. Some of these traits are quite positive—for instance, our ability to cooperate with one another in a group—while some of them are negative and can prove destructive. Most of us have these negative qualities—*Envy*, *Conformism*, *Rigidity*, *Self-obsessiveness*, *Laziness*, *Flightiness*, and *Passive Aggression*—in relatively mild doses. But in a group setting, there will inevitably be people who have one or more of these qualities to a high enough degree that they can become very destructive. We shall call these negative qualities the *Seven Deadly Realities*.

Through study and observation, we must understand the nature of these Seven Deadly Realities so that we can detect their presence and avoid triggering them in the first place. Consider the following as essential knowledge in acquiring social intelligence.

Envy: It is our nature to constantly compare ourselves to others—in terms of money, looks, coolness, intelligence, popularity, or any number of categories. If we are upset that someone we know is more successful than we are, we will naturally experience some envy. But for some people it goes much deeper than this, usually because of the level of their insecurities. Seething with envy, the only way to discharge it is to find a way to obstruct or sabotage the person who elicited the emotion. If they take such action they will *never* say it is because of envy, but will find some other, more socially acceptable excuse. This makes it a quality very hard to recognize in people. There are, however, a few indications you can look for. People who praise you too much or who become overly friendly in the first stages of knowing you are often envious and are getting closer in order to hurt you. Also, if you detect unusual levels of insecurity in a person, he or she will certainly be more prone to envy.

In general, however, envy is very difficult to discern, and the most prudent course of action is to make sure your own behavior does not inadvertently trigger it. If you have a gift for a certain skill, you should make a point of occasionally displaying some weakness in another area, avoiding the great danger of appearing too perfect, too talented. If you are dealing with insecure types, you can display great interest in *their* work and even turn to them for advice.

Conformism: When people form groups of any type, a kind of organizational mind-set inevitably sets in. Although members of the group might trumpet their tolerance and celebration of people's differences, the reality is that those who are markedly different make them feel uncomfortable and insecure, calling the values of the dominant culture into question.

If you have a rebellious or naturally eccentric streak, as is often the case with those who are aiming for mastery, you must be careful in displaying your difference too overtly, particularly in the Apprenticeship Phase. Let your work subtly demonstrate your individual spirit, but when it comes to matters of politics, morals, and values, make a show of adhering to the accepted standards of your environment. Later, as you gain mastery, you will have ample opportunity to let your individuality shine through and to reveal your contempt for people's correctness.

Rigidity: The world has become increasingly complex in many ways, and whenever we humans face a situation that seems complicated our response is to resort to a kind of artificial simplicity, to create habits and routines that give us a sense of control. We prefer what is familiar.

This extends to the group at large. People follow procedures without really knowing why, simply because these procedures may have worked in the past, and they become highly defensive if their ways are brought into question.

It is useless to fight against people's rigid ways, or to argue against their irrational concepts. You will only waste time and make yourself rigid in the process. The best strategy is to simply accept rigidity in others, outwardly displaying deference to their need for order. On your own, however, you must work to maintain your open spirit, letting go of bad habits and deliberately cultivating new ideas.

Self-obsessiveness: In the work environment, we almost inevitably think first and foremost of ourselves. The world is a harsh and competitive place, and we must look after our own interests. Even when we act for the greater good, we are often unconsciously motivated by the desire to be liked by others and to have our image enhanced in the process.

You must understand and accept this Deadly Reality. When it is time to ask for a favor or help, you must think first of appealing to people's self-interest in some way. You must look at the world through their eyes, getting a sense of their needs. You must give them something valuable in exchange for helping you. In general, in your interactions with people, find a way to make the conversations revolve around them and their interests, all of which will go far to winning them to your side.

Laziness: We all have the tendency to want to take

the quickest, easiest path to our goals, but we generally manage to control our impatience; we understand the superior value of getting what we want through hard work. For some people, however, this inveterate lazy streak is far too powerful. Discouraged by the thought that it might take months or years to get somewhere, they are constantly on the lookout for shortcuts. If you are not careful and talk too much, they will steal your best ideas and make them their own, saving themselves all of the mental effort that went into conceiving them. They will swoop in during the middle of your project and put their name on it, gaining partial credit for your work. They will engage you in a "collaboration" in which you do the bulk of the hard work but they share equally in the rewards.

Your best defense is your prudence. Keep your ideas to yourself, or conceal enough of the details so that it is not possible to steal them. If you are doing work for a superior, be prepared for them to take full credit and leave your name out, but do not let this happen with colleagues. In general, be wary of people who want to collaborate—they are often trying to find someone who will do the heavier lifting for them.

Flightiness: We like to make a show of how much our decisions are based on rational considerations, but the truth is that we are largely governed by our emotions, which continually color our perceptions. What this means is that the people around you, constantly under the pull of their emotions, change their ideas by the day or by the hour, depending on their mood.

It is best to cultivate both distance and a degree of detachment from other people's shifting emotions so that you are not caught up in the process. Do not take so seriously people's promises or their ardor in wanting to help you. Rely upon yourself to get things done and you will not be disappointed.

Passive Aggression: The root cause of all passive aggression is the human fear of direct confrontation. Because of this fear some people look for indirect means for getting their way, making their attacks subtle enough so that it is hard to figure out what is going on, while giving them control of the dynamic. We are all passive-aggressive to some extent. But there are people out there seething with insecurities who are veritable passive-aggressive warriors and can literally ruin your life.

Your best defense is to recognize such types before you become embroiled in a battle, and avoid them like the plague. The most obvious clues come from their track record—they have a reputation, you hear stories of past skirmishes, and so on. If they evade you and delay necessary action on something important to you, or make you feel guilty and leave you unsure why, or if they act harmfully but make it seem like an accident, you are most likely under a passive-aggressive attack. At all cost, avoid entangling yourself emotionally in their dramas and battles. They are masters at controlling the dynamic, and you will almost always lose in the end.

STRATEGIES FOR ACQUIRING SOCIAL INTELLIGENCE

> *We must, however, acknowledge . . . that man with all his noble qualities, with sympathy which feels for the most debased, with benevolence which extends not only to other men but to the humblest living creature, with his god-like intellect which has penetrated into the movements and constitution of the solar system—with all these exalted powers—Man still bears in his bodily frame the indelible stamp of his lowly origin.*
>
> —CHARLES DARWIN

In dealing with people, you will often encounter particular problems that will tend to make you emotional and lock you into the Naïve Perspective. Such problems include unexpected political battles, superficial judgments of your character based on appearances, or petty-minded criticisms of your work. The following four essential strategies, developed by Masters past and present, will help you to meet these inevitable challenges and maintain the rational mind-set necessary for social intelligence.

1. Speak through your work

Your work is the single greatest means at your disposal for expressing your social intelligence. By being efficient and detail oriented in what you do, you *demonstrate* that you are thinking of the group at large and advancing its cause. By making what you write or present clear and easy to follow, you *show* your care for the audience or public at large. By involving other people in your projects and gracefully accepting their feedback, you *reveal* your comfort with the group dynamic. Work that is solid also protects you from the political conniving and malevolence of others—it is hard to argue with the results you produce. If you are experiencing the pressures of political maneuvering within the group, do not lose your head and become consumed with all of the pettiness. By remaining focused and speaking socially through your work, you will both continue to raise your skill level *and* stand out among all the others who make a lot of noise but produce nothing.

2. Craft the appropriate persona

People will tend to judge you based on your outward appearance. If you are not careful and simply assume that it is best to be yourself, they will begin to ascribe to you all kinds of qualities that have little to do with who you are but correspond to what they want to see. All of this can confuse you, make you feel insecure, and consume your attention. Internalizing their judgments, you will find it hard to focus on your work. Your only protection is to turn this dynamic around by consciously molding these appearances, creating the image that suits you, and controlling people's judgments. At times you will find it appropriate to stand back and create some mystery around you, heightening your presence. At other times you will want to be more direct and impose a more specific appearance. In general, you never settle on one image or give people the power to completely figure you out. You are always one step ahead of the public.

You must see the creation of a persona as a key element in social intelligence, not something evil or demonic. We all wear masks in the social arena, playing different roles to suit the different environments we pass through. You are simply becoming more conscious of the process. Think of it as theater. By creating a persona that is mysterious, intriguing, and masterful, you are playing to the public, giving them something compelling and pleasurable to witness. You are allowing them to project their fantasies onto you. You must take pleasure in creating these personas—it will make you a better performer on the public stage.

3. See yourself as others see you

Almost all of us have social flaws of some sort, ranging from the relatively harmless to those that can get us in trouble. Perhaps it could be that we talk too much, or are too honest in our criticisms of people, or take offense too easily when others do not respond positively to our ideas. If we repeat instances of such behavior often enough, we tend to offend people without ever really knowing why. The reason for this is twofold: first, we are quick to discern the mistakes and defects of others, but when it comes to ourselves we are generally too emotional and insecure to look squarely at our own. Second, people rarely tell us the truth about what it is that we do wrong. They are afraid to cause conflict or to be viewed as mean-spirited. And so it becomes very difficult for us to perceive our flaws, let alone correct them.

To have the power to see ourselves through the eyes of others would be of immense benefit to our social intelligence. We could begin to correct the flaws that offend, to see the role that we play in creating any kind of negative dynamic, and to have a more realistic assessment of who we are. We can begin this process by looking at negative events in our past—people sabotaging our work, bosses firing us for no logical reason, nasty personal battles with colleagues. In dissecting these occurrences, we must focus on what *we* did that either triggered or worsened the dynamic. In looking at several such incidents, we might begin to see a pattern that indicates a particular flaw in our character. Seeing these events from the perspective of the other people involved will loosen the lock our emotions have on our self-image, and help us understand the role we play in our own mistakes. We can also elicit opinions from those we trust about our behavior, making certain to first reassure them that we want their criticisms. Slowly, in this way, we can develop increasing self-detachment, which will yield us the other half of social intelligence—the ability to see ourselves as we really are.

4. Suffer fools gladly

In the course of your life you will be continually encountering fools. There are simply too many to avoid. We can classify people as fools by the following rubric: when it comes to practical life, what should matter is getting long-term results, and getting the work done in as efficient and creative a manner as possible. That should be the supreme value that guides people's actions. But fools carry with them a different scale of values. They place more importance on short-term matters—grabbing immediate money, getting attention from the public or media, and looking good. They are ruled by their ego and insecurities. They tend to enjoy drama and political intrigue for their own sake. When they criticize, they always emphasize matters that are irrelevant to the overall picture or argument. They are more interested in their career and position than in the truth. You can distinguish them by how little they get done, or by how hard they make it for others to get results. They lack a certain common sense, getting worked up about things that are not really important while ignoring problems that will spell doom in the long term.

The natural tendency with fools is to lower yourself to their level. They annoy you, get under your skin, and draw you into a battle. In the process, you feel petty and confused. You lose a sense of what is really important. You can't win an argument or get them to see your side or change their behavior, because rationality and results don't matter to them. You simply waste valuable time and emotional energy.

In dealing with fools you must adopt the following philosophy: they are simply a part of life, like rocks or furniture. All of us have foolish sides, moments in which we lose our heads and think more of our ego or short-term goals. It is human nature. Seeing this foolishness within you, you can then accept it in others. This will allow you to smile at their antics, to tolerate their presence as you would a silly child, and to avoid the madness of trying to change them. It is all part of the human comedy, and it is nothing to get upset about or lose sleep over. This attitude—"Suffer Fools Gladly"—should be forged in your Apprenticeship Phase, during which you are almost certainly going to encounter this type. If they are causing you trouble, you must neutralize the harm they do by keeping a steady eye on your goals and what is important, and ignoring them if you can. The height of wisdom, however, is to take this even further and to actually exploit their foolishness—using them for material for your work, as examples of things to avoid, or by looking for ways to turn their actions to your advantage. In this way, their foolishness plays into your hands, helping you achieve the kind of practical results they seem to disdain.

V

AWAKEN THE DIMENSIONAL MIND: THE CREATIVE-ACTIVE

As you accumulate more skills and internalize the rules that govern your field, your mind will want to become more active, seeking to use this knowledge in ways that are more suited to your inclinations. What will impede this natural creative dynamic from flourishing is not a lack of talent, but your attitude. Feeling anxious and insecure, you will tend to turn conservative with your knowledge, preferring to fit into the group and sticking to the procedures you have learned. Instead, you must force yourself in the opposite direction. Instead of feeling complacent about what you know, you must expand your knowledge to related fields, giving your mind fuel to make new associations between different ideas. You must experiment and look at problems from all possible angles. As your thinking grows more fluid your mind will become increasingly dimensional, seeing more and more aspects of reality.

THE SECOND TRANSFORMATION

From the moment he was born, Wolfgang Amadeus Mozart (1756–91) was surrounded by music. His father, Leopold, was a violinist and composer in the court of Salzburg, Austria, as well as a music instructor. All during the day, Wolfgang would hear Leopold and his students practicing in the house. In 1759, his seven-year-old sister Maria Anna began taking piano lessons from their father. She showed great promise and practiced at all hours. Wolfgang, enchanted by the simple melodies that she played, began to hum along to the music; he would sometimes sit at the family's harpsichord and try to imitate what his sister had played. Leopold could soon detect something unusual in his son. For a three-year-old, the child had a remarkable memory for melody and an impeccable sense of rhythm, all without having had any instruction.

Although he had never attempted to teach someone so young, Leopold decided to begin teaching piano to Wolfgang when he turned four, and after only a few sessions he realized the boy had other interesting qualities. Wolfgang listened more deeply than other students, his mind and body completely absorbed in the music. With such intensity of focus, he learned more quickly than other children. Once when he was five years old, he stole a rather complicated exercise meant for Maria Anna, and within thirty minutes he could play it with ease. He had heard Maria Anna practice the piece, and remembering it vividly, the moment he saw the notes on the page he could rapidly reproduce the music.

This remarkable focus had its roots in something that Leopold saw almost from the beginning—the boy had an intense love of music itself. His eyes would light up with excitement the moment Leopold laid out a new challenging piece for him to conquer. If the piece was new and hard to figure out, he would attack it day and night with such tenacity that it would soon become part of his repertoire. At night, his parents would have to force him to stop practicing and send him to bed. This love of practice only seemed to increase with the years.

One day in 1762, as Leopold Mozart heard his two children playing a piece for two pianos, an idea came to him. His daughter Maria Anna was a very talented piano player in her own right, and Wolfgang was a veritable marvel. Together, they were like precious toys. They had a natural charisma, and Wolfgang had a showman's flair. As a mere court musician, Leopold's income was rather limited, but he could see the potential for making a fortune through his children. And so, thinking this through, he decided to take his family on a grand tour of the capitals of Europe, playing before royal courts and the public and charging money for the entertainment. To add to the spectacle, he dressed the children up—Maria Anna as a princess, and Wolfgang as a court minister, complete with wig, elaborate waistcoat, and a sword dangling from his belt.

They began in Vienna, where the children charmed the Austrian emperor and empress. They then spent months in Paris, where they played for the royal court and Wolfgang bounced on the knee of the delighted

King Louis XV. They continued to London where they ended up staying for over a year, playing before all kinds of large crowds. And while the sight of the two children in their costumes charmed audiences enough, Wolfgang's playing astounded them. He would play his own compositions—it was impressive to hear a sonata composed by a seven-year-old, no matter how simple it was. Most marvelous of all, Wolfgang could play at an incredible speed, his tiny fingers flying over the keyboard.

As the tour continued, Wolfgang developed the habit of attaching himself to the most illustrious composer in the particular court they were visiting. In London, for instance, he managed to charm the great composer Johann Christian Bach, son of Johann Sebastian Bach. The education he received in this fashion, from all of the composers he met, went far beyond anything any child could hope to receive.

The Mozart family had come now to depend on the money that the children had generated through the tour, but as the years went by the invitations began to dry up. The novelty had worn off, and the children no longer seemed so young and precious. Desperate to generate money, Leopold came up with a different scheme. His son was turning into a serious composer, with the ability to compose in different genres. What was needed was to secure for him a stable position as a court composer, and attract commissions for concertos and symphonies. With this goal in mind, in 1770 father and son embarked on series of tours of Italy, then the center of all things musical in Europe.

The trip went well. Wolfgang performed his magic on the piano before all of the major courts in Italy. He gained acclaim for his symphonies and concert pieces—they were quite impressive for a teenager. He mingled yet again with the most celebrated composers of his time, intensifying the musical knowledge he had gained on his previous tours. In addition, he rediscovered his greatest passion in music—the opera. As a child he had always had the feeling that he was destined to compose great operas. In Italy he saw the finest productions and realized the source of his fascination—it was the drama translated into pure music, the nearly limitless potential of the human voice to express the full range of emotion, and the overall spectacle. He had an almost primal attraction to any kind of theater. But despite all of the attention and inspiration he received, after nearly three years of visiting the various courts in Italy, he was not offered a position or a commission that was worthy of his talents. And so, in 1773, father and son returned to Salzburg.

After some delicate negotiation with the archbishop of Salzburg, Leopold finally managed to secure for his son a relatively lucrative position as court musician and composer. And by all appearances the arrangement was good: not having to worry about money, Wolfgang would have endless time to work on composing. But almost from the beginning Wolfgang felt uncomfortable and restless. He had spent almost half of his youth traveling throughout Europe, mingling with the leading minds in music, and listening to the most renowned orchestras, and now he was relegated to life in provincial

Salzburg, isolated from the European centers of music, in a city that had no theater or opera tradition.

More troubling, however, was the mounting frustration he felt as a composer. For as long as he could remember, his head was continuously filled with music, but it was always the music of other people. He knew that his own pieces were simply clever imitations and adaptations of other composers. He had been like a young plant, passively absorbing nutrients from the environment in the form of the different styles he had learned and mastered. But he could feel stirring from deep within something more active, the desire to express his own music and to stop imitating. The soil was now rich enough. As an adolescent, he was assailed by all kinds of conflicting and powerful emotions—elation, depression, erotic desires. His great desire was to transpose these feelings into his work.

Almost without being aware of it, he began to experiment. He wrote a series of slow movements for various string quartets that were long and drawn out with strange mixes of moods, full of anxiety that would rise to great crescendos. When he showed these pieces to his father, Leopold was horrified. Their income depended on Wolfgang supplying the court with the kind of pleasant melodies that would delight people. If they or the archbishop heard these new compositions, they would think Wolfgang had gone insane. Besides, the pieces were too complicated for the court musicians of Salzburg to perform. He begged his son to stop indulging in such strange music.

Wolfgang acquiesced, but as time went on he grew increasingly depressed. For the first time in his life he was losing his love for music itself. Feeling imprisoned, he grew irritable. Slowly he resigned himself to his fate: he would die in Salzburg at an early age, without the world ever hearing the kind of music he knew existed within him.

In 1781 Wolfgang was invited to accompany the archbishop of Salzburg to Vienna, where he was planning to showcase the musical talents of his various court musicians. Suddenly, in Vienna, the nature of his status as a court musician became clear. The archbishop ordered him about as if he were simply one of his personal staff, a mere servant. Now all the resentment Wolfgang had felt for the past seven years bubbled and rose to the surface. He was twenty-five years old and losing valuable time. His father and the archbishop were actively holding him back. He loved his father and depended on his family for emotional support, but he could tolerate his circumstances no longer. When it was time to return to Salzburg, he did the unthinkable—he refused to leave. He asked to be dismissed from his position. The archbishop treated him with the utmost contempt, but finally relented. His father sided with the archbishop and ordered his son to return, promising that all would be forgiven. But Wolfgang had made up his mind: he would stay in Vienna, for what would turn out to be the rest of his life.

The rift with his father was permanent and extremely painful, but sensing that his time was short and that he had almost too much to express, he threw himself into his music with an intensity that was even greater than what he had displayed in childhood. As if all of his ideas had been pent up for too long, he exploded in a creative outburst unprecedented in the history of music.

The apprenticeship of the past twenty years had prepared him well for this moment. He had developed a prodigious memory—in his mind he could hold together all of the harmonies and melodies that he had absorbed over the years. Instead of notes or chords, he could think in terms of blocks of music and write them out as quickly as he heard them in his head.

He gave his compositions the power to convey dread, sadness, foreboding, anger, exhilaration, and ecstasy. Audiences were spellbound by this new sweeping sound that suddenly had so many new dimensions. After these innovations, it became almost impossible for composers to return to the light, frothy court music that had previously prevailed. European music had forever been altered.

These innovations did not spring from any conscious desire on his part to provoke or rebel. Rather, his transforming spirit emerged as if it were completely natural and beyond his control, like a bee secreting wax. Aided by his superior sense of music, he simply could not help but personalize every genre he worked in.

In 1786 he came upon a version of the Don Juan legend that excited him. He immediately identified with the story of the great seducer. He shared Don Juan's obsessive need and love for women, and he had the same disdain for authority figures. But more important, Mozart felt that as a composer he had the supreme ability to seduce audiences and that music itself represented the ultimate seduction, with its irresistible power to strike at our emotions. Translating this story into an opera, he could convey all of these ideas. And so the following year he began early work on his opera *Don Giovanni* (Italian for Don Juan). To make this story come alive in the way he had imagined it, he would once again apply his transformative powers—this time to the genre of opera.

At the time, operas tended to be rather static and formulaic. They consisted of recitatives (spoken dialogue accompanied by harpsichord that conveyed the story and action), arias (sung portions in which the singer would react to the information in the recitative), and choral pieces, featuring large groups of people singing together. For his opera, Mozart created something that flowed as a continuous whole. He conveyed the character of Don Giovanni not just through the words but through the music, accompanying the seducer's presence on stage with a constant twitching tremolo in the violins to represent his nervous, sensual energy. He gave the work an accelerated, almost frantic pace that no one had ever witnessed before in the theater. To push the expressive value of the music further, he invented ensembles—stirring, climactic moments in which several characters would sing, sometimes over one another, in an elaborate counterpoint, giving the opera a dreamlike feel and flow.

From beginning to end, *Don Giovanni* resonated

with the demonic presence of the great seducer. Although all of the other characters condemn him, it is impossible not to admire Don Giovanni even as he remains unrepentant to the end, laughing all the way to hell and refusing to submit to authority. *Don Giovanni* was not like any opera anyone had ever seen before, either in the story or in the music, and it was perhaps too far ahead of its time. Many complained that it was all rather ugly and harsh to the ears; they found the pace too frenetic and the moral ambiguity too disturbing.

Continuing to work at a deliriously creative pace, Mozart exhausted himself and died in 1791, two months after the premier of his last opera, *The Magic Flute*, at the age of thirty-five. Several years after his death audiences caught up with the radical sound he had created in works such as *Don Giovanni*, which soon became among the five most frequently performed operas in history.

KEYS TO MASTERY

> . . . *Several things dovetailed in my mind, & at once it struck me, what quality went to form a Man of Achievement especially in Literature & which Shakespeare possessed so enormously—I mean Negative Capability, that is when man is capable of being in uncertainties, Mysteries, doubts, without any irritable reaching after fact & reason.* . . .
>
> —JOHN KEATS

If we think deeply about our childhood, not just about our memories of it but how it actually felt, we realize how differently we experienced the world back then. Our minds were completely open, and we entertained all kinds of surprising, original ideas. Things that we now take for granted often caused us to wonder. Our heads teemed with questions about the world around us. Not yet having commanded language, we thought in ways that were preverbal—in images and sensations. When we attended the circus, a sporting event, or a movie, our eyes and ears took in the spectacle with utmost intensity. Colors seemed more vibrant and alive. We had a powerful desire to turn everything around us into a game, to play with circumstances.

Let us call this quality the *Original Mind*. This mind looked at the world more directly—not through words and received ideas. It was flexible and receptive to new information. Retaining a memory of this *Original Mind*, we cannot help but feel nostalgia for the intensity with which we used to experience the world. As the years pass, this intensity inevitably diminishes. We come to see the world through a screen of words and opinions; our prior experiences, layered over the present, color what we see. We no longer look at things as they are, noticing their details, or wonder why they exist. Our minds gradually tighten up. We become defensive about the world we now take for granted, and we become upset if our beliefs or assumptions are attacked.

We can call this way of thinking the *Conventional Mind*. Under pressure to make a living and conform to society, we force our minds into tighter and tighter grooves.

Masters, and those who display a high level of creative energy, are simply people who manage to retain a sizeable portion of their childhood spirit despite the pressures and demands of adulthood. This spirit manifests itself in their work and in their ways of thinking. Children are naturally creative. They actively transform everything around them, play with ideas and circumstances, and surprise us with the novel things they say or do. But the natural creativity of children is limited; it never leads to discoveries, inventions, or substantial works of art.

Masters not only retain the spirit of the *Original Mind*, but they add to it their years of apprenticeship and an ability to focus deeply on problems or ideas. This leads to high-level creativity. Although they have profound knowledge of a subject, their minds remain open to alternative ways of seeing and approaching problems. They retain a childlike excitement about their field and a playful approach.

Some people maintain their childlike spirit and spontaneity, but their creative energy is dissipated in a thousand directions, and they never have the patience and discipline to endure an extended apprenticeship. Others have the discipline to accumulate vast amounts of knowledge and become experts in their field, but they have no flexibility of spirit, so their ideas never stray beyond the conventional and they never become truly creative. Masters manage to blend the two—discipline and a childlike spirit—together into what we shall call the *Dimensional Mind*. Such a mind is not constricted by limited experience or habits. It can branch out in all directions and make deep contact with reality. It can explore more dimensions of the world. It is active, transforming everything it digests into something new and original, *creating* instead of *consuming*.

Understand: we all possess an inborn creative force that wants to become active. This is the gift of our *Original Mind*, which reveals such potential. The human mind is naturally creative, constantly looking to make associations and connections between things and ideas. What kills the creative force is not age or a lack of talent, but our own spirit, our own attitude. We become too comfortable with the knowledge we have gained in our apprenticeships. We grow afraid of entertaining new ideas and the effort that this requires.

What this means, however, is that we equally possess the potential to spark this innate creative force back to life, no matter how old we are. By understanding how the *Dimensional Mind* operates and what helps it flourish, we can consciously revive our mental elasticity and reverse the deadening process. The powers that the *Dimensional Mind* can bring are nearly limitless, and within the reach of almost all of us.

Look at the case of Wolfgang Amadeus Mozart. He is generally considered the epitome of the child prodigy and the inexplicable genius, a freak of nature. How else are we to explain his uncanny abilities at such a young age, and the ten-year burst of creative activity at the end of his life that culminated in so many innovations and universally loved works? In truth, his genius and creativity is eminently explicable, which does not at all diminish his achievements.

Immersed in and enchanted by music from the very beginning of his life, he brought to his earliest studies a high level of focus and intensity. The mind of a four-year-old is even more open and impressionable than that of a child a few years older. Much of this powerful attention stemmed from his deep love of music. And so practicing the piano was not some kind of chore or duty, but an opportunity to expand his knowledge and to explore more musical possibilities. By the age of six, he had accumulated the hours of practice of someone twice his age. The years of touring exposed him to every possible trend and innovation of his time. His mind became filled with an extensive vocabulary of forms and styles.

In his adolescence Mozart experienced a typical creative crisis. For close to eight years, under pressure from his father, he had to temper his own powerful creative urges. At this critical point he could have succumbed to this dampening of his spirit and continued to write relatively tame pieces for the court. Instead he rebelled and reconnected with his childlike spirit—that original desire of his to transform the music into his own voice, to realize his dramatic urges in opera. With all of his pent-up energy, his long apprenticeship, the deep level of his knowledge, he naturally exploded with creativity once he had freed himself from his family. The speed with which he could compose such masterpieces is not a reflection of some divine gift, but rather of how powerfully his mind had come to think in musical terms, which he could translate easily onto paper. He was not a freak, but a signpost of the outer reaches of the creative potential we all naturally possess.

The *Dimensional Mind* has two essential requirements: one, a high level of knowledge about a field or subject; and two, the openness and flexibility to use this knowledge in new and original ways. The knowledge that prepares the ground for creative activity largely comes from a rigorous apprenticeship in which we have mastered all of the basics. Once the mind is freed from having to learn these basics, it can focus on higher, more creative matters. The problem for us all is that the knowledge we gain in the Apprenticeship Phase—including numerous rules and procedures—can slowly become a prison. It locks us into certain methods and forms of thinking that are one-dimensional. Instead, the mind must be forced from its conservative positions and made active and exploratory.

To awaken the *Dimensional Mind* and move through the creative process requires three essential steps: first, choosing the proper *Creative Task*, the kind of activity that will maximize our skills and knowledge; second, loosening and opening up the mind through certain *Creative Strategies;* and third, creating the optimal mental conditions for a *Breakthrough* or *Insight*. Finally, throughout the process we must also be aware of the *Emotional Pitfalls*—complacency, boredom, grandiosity, and the like—that continually threaten to derail or block our progress. If we can move through the steps while avoiding these traps, we cannot fail to unleash powerful creative forces from within.

Step One: The Creative Task

You must begin by altering your very concept of creativity and by trying to see it from a new angle. To make a discovery, to invent something that connects with the public, to fashion a work of art that is meaningful, inevitably requires time and effort. This often entails years of experimentation, various setbacks and failures, and the need to maintain a high level of focus. You must have patience and faith that what you are doing will yield something important. You could have the most brilliant mind, teeming with knowledge and ideas, but if you choose the wrong subject or problem to attack, you can run out of energy and interest. In such a case all of your intellectual brilliance will lead to nothing. The task that you choose to work on must have an obsessive element. Like the Life's Task, it must connect to something deep within you.

Understand: it is the choice of where to direct his or her creative energy that makes the Master.

This is *The Primary Law of the Creative Dynamic* that you must engrave deeply in your mind and never forget: your emotional commitment to what you are doing will be translated directly into your work. If you go at your work with half a heart, it will show in the lackluster results. If you are doing something primarily for money and without a real emotional commitment, it will translate into something that lacks a soul and that has no connection to you. You may not see this, but you can be sure that the public will feel it and that they will receive your work in the same lackluster spirit it was created in. If you are excited and obsessive in the hunt, it will show in the details. If your work comes from a place deep within, its authenticity will be communicated. This applies equally to science and business as to the arts. You must never simply embark on any creative endeavor in your field, placing faith in your own brilliance to see it through. You must make the right, the perfect choice for your energies and your inclinations.

To aid in this process, it is often wise to choose something that appeals to your sense of unconventionality and calls up latent feelings of rebelliousness. Perhaps what you want to invent or discover is being ignored or ridiculed by others. In opting for something that has deep personal appeal to you, you will naturally move in an unorthodox direction. Try to ally this with a desire to subvert conventional paradigms and go against the grain. The sense of having enemies or doubters can serve as a powerful motivating device and fill you with an added creative energy and focus.

There are two things to keep in mind: First, the task that you choose must be realistic. The knowledge and skills you have gained must be eminently suited to pulling it off.

Second, you must let go of your need for comfort and security. Creative endeavors are by their nature uncertain. You may know your task, but you are never exactly sure where your efforts will lead. If you need everything in your life to be simple and safe, this open-ended nature of the task will fill you with anxiety. If you are worried about what others might think and about how your position in the group might be jeopardized, then you will never really create anything. If you are worried about failure or going through a period of mental and financial instability, then you will violate the Primary Law of the Creative Dynamic, and your worries will be reflected in the results. Think of yourself as an explorer. You cannot find anything new if you are unwilling to leave the shore.

Step Two: Creative Strategies

Think of the mind as a muscle that naturally tightens up over time unless it is consciously worked upon. What causes this tightening is twofold. First, we generally prefer to entertain the same thoughts and ways of thinking because they provide us with a sense of consistency and familiarity. Sticking with the same methods also saves us a lot of effort. We are creatures of habit. Second, whenever we work hard at a problem or idea, our minds naturally narrow their focus because of the strain and effort involved. This means that the further we progress on our creative task, the fewer alternative possibilities or viewpoints we tend to consider.

This tightening process afflicts all of us. The only antidote is to enact strategies to loosen up the mind and let in alternative ways of thinking. The following five strategies for developing such flexibility have been distilled from the lessons and stories of the most creative Masters, past and present. It would be wise to adapt all of them at some point, stretching and loosening the mind in all directions.

A. CULTIVATE NEGATIVE CAPABILITY

We are by nature fearful and insecure creatures. We do not like what is unfamiliar or unknown. To compensate for this, we assert ourselves with opinions and ideas that make us seem strong and certain. Many of these opinions do not come from our own deep reflection, but are instead based on what other people think. Furthermore, once we hold these ideas, to admit they are wrong is to wound our ego and vanity. Truly creative people in all fields can temporarily suspend their ego and simply experience what they are seeing, without the need to assert a judgment, for as long as possible. They are more than ready to find their most cherished opinions contradicted by reality. This ability to endure and even embrace mysteries and uncertainties is what the great English poet John Keats called *negative capability*.

All Masters possess this Negative Capability, and it is the source of their creative power. This quality allows them to entertain a broader range of ideas and experiment with them, which in turn makes their work richer and more inventive.

To put Negative Capability into practice, you must develop the habit of suspending the need to judge everything that crosses your path. You consider and even momentarily entertain viewpoints opposite to your own. You observe a person or event for a length of time, deliberately holding yourself back from forming an opinion. You seek out what is unfamiliar. You do anything to break up your normal train of thinking and your sense that you already know the truth.

Negative Capability should not be a permanent state of mind. In order to produce work of any sort we must create limits on what we'll consider; we must organize our thoughts into relatively cohesive patterns, and eventually, come up with conclusions. In the end, we must make certain judgments. Negative Capability is a tool we use in the process to open the mind up temporarily to more possibilities.

B. ALLOW FOR SERENDIPITY

The brain is an instrument developed for making connections. It operates as a dual processing system, in which every bit of information that comes in is at the same time compared to other information. The brain is constantly searching for similarities, differences, and relationships between what it processes. Your task is to feed this natural inclination, to create the optimal conditions for it to make new and original associations between ideas and experiences. And one of the best ways to accomplish this is by letting go of conscious control and allowing chance to enter into the process.

The reason for this is simple. When we are consumed with a particular project, our attention tends to become quite narrow as we focus so deeply. We grow tense. In this state, our mind responds by trying to reduce the amount of stimuli we have to deal with. We literally close ourselves off from the world in order to concentrate on what is necessary. This can have the un-intended consequence of making it harder for us to see other possibilities, to be more open and creative with our ideas. When we are in a more relaxed state, our at-tention naturally broadens and we take in more stimuli.

Many of the most interesting and profound discov-eries in science occur when the thinker is not concentrat-ing directly on the problem but is about to drift off to sleep, or get on a bus, or hears a joke—moments of un-strained attention, when something unexpected enters the mental sphere and triggers a new and fertile connec-tion. Such chance associations and discoveries are known as *serendipity*—the occurrence of something we are not expecting—and although by their nature you cannot force them to happen, you can invite serendipity into the creative process by taking two simple steps.

The first step is to widen your search as far as pos-sible. In the research stage of your project, you look at more than what is generally required. You expand your search into other fields, reading and absorbing any re-lated information. If you have a particular theory or hypothesis about a phenomenon, you examine as many examples and potential counterexamples as humanly possible. It might seem tiring and inefficient, but you must trust this process. What ensues is that the brain becomes increasingly excited and stimulated by the variety of information. A kind of mental momentum is generated, in which the slightest chance occurrence will spark a fertile idea.

The second step is to maintain an openness and looseness of spirit. In moments of great tension and searching, you allow yourself moments of release. You take walks, engage in activities outside your work, or think about something else, no matter how trivial. When some new and unanticipated idea now enters your mind, you do not ignore it because it is irrational or does not fit the narrow frame of your previous work. You give it instead full attention and explore where it leads you.

To help yourself to cultivate serendipity, you should keep a notebook with you at all times. The moment any idea or observation comes, you note it down. In this notebook you record any scrap of thought that occurs to you, and include drawings, quotes from other books, anything at all. In this way, you will have the freedom to try out the most absurd ideas. The juxtaposition of so many random bits will be enough to spark various associations.

In general you must adopt a more *analogical way* of thinking, taking greater advantage of the associative powers of the mind. Thinking in terms of analogies and metaphors can be extremely helpful to the creative process.

These analogies can be tight and logical, such as Isaac Newton's comparison of the falling apple from a tree in his garden to the moon falling in space. Or they can be loose and somewhat irrational, such as the jazz artist John Coltrane's thinking of his own compositions as cathedrals of sound he was constructing. In any event, you must train yourself to look constantly for such analogies to reframe and expand your ideas.

C. ALTERNATE THE MIND THROUGH "THE CURRENT"

The Current is like a mental electrical charge that gains its power through a constant alternation. We observe something in the world that strikes our attention and makes us wonder what it might mean. In thinking about it, we devise several possible explanations. When we look at the phenomenon again we see it differently as we cycle through the various ideas we had imagined to account for it. Perhaps we conduct experiments to verify or alter our speculations. Now when we look at the phenomenon yet again, weeks or months later, we see more and more aspects of its hidden reality.

If we had failed to speculate on the meaning of what we had observed, we simply would have had an observation that led us nowhere. If we had speculated without continuing to observe and verify, then we simply would have had some random idea floating in our heads. But by continually cycling between speculation and observation/experiment, we are able to pierce deeper and deeper into reality, like a drill that penetrates a piece of wood through its motion. The Current is a constant dialogue between our thoughts and reality. If we go into this process deeply enough, we come into contact with a theory that explains something far beyond the capability of our limited senses.

Most often in culture we see people who *short-circuit* the Current. They observe some phenomenon in culture or nature that makes them emotional and they run rampant with speculations, never taking the time to entertain possible explanations that could have been verified by further observation. On the other hand, we see many people, particularly in academia or in the sciences, who accumulate mountains of information and data from studies and statistics but never venture to speculate on the larger ramifications of this information or connect it all into a theory. Instead, you must follow the route of all creative thinkers and go in the opposite direction. You not only speculate, but are bold and audacious with your ideas, all of which forces you to work hard to confirm or disconfirm your theories, piercing into reality in the process. As the great physicist Max Planck put it, scientists "must have a vivid intuitive imagination, for new ideas are not generated by deduction, but by an artistically creative imagination."

The Current can be applied to any kind of new invention or business idea, by working with artifacts or prototypes. Let us say you have an idea for a new product. You can design it on your own and then launch it, but often you notice a discrepancy between your own level of excitement for your product and the somewhat indifferent response of the public. You have not engaged in a dialogue with reality, which is the essence of the Current. Instead, it is better to produce a prototype—a form of speculation—and see how people respond to it. Based on the assessments you gain, you can redo the work and launch it again, cycling through this process several times until you perfect it. The responses of the public will make you think more deeply about what you are producing. Such feedback will help make visible what is generally invisible to your eyes—the objective reality of your work and its flaws, as reflected through the eyes of many people. Alternating between ideas and artifacts will help you to create something compelling and effective.

D. ALTER YOUR PERSPECTIVE

Consider thinking as an extended form of vision that allows us to see more of the world, and creativity as the ability to expand that vision beyond conventional boundaries.

When we perceive an object, our eyes relay only a portion or outline of it to our brains, leaving our mind to fill in the rest, giving us a fast and relatively accurate assessment of what we are seeing. Our eyes are not paying deep attention to all of the details, but noticing patterns. Our thought processes, modeled after visual perception, use a similar shorthand. When an event occurs or when we meet a new person, we do not stop to consider all aspects or details, but instead we see an outline or pattern that fits into our expectations and past experiences. We fit the event or person into categories.

Creative people are those who have the capacity to resist this shorthand. They can look at a phenomenon from several different angles, noticing something we miss because we only look straight on. Whether such powers are natural or learned does not matter: the mind can be trained to loosen itself up and move outside the grooves. To do this you must become aware of the typical patterns your mind falls into and how you can break out of these patterns and alter your perspective through conscious effort. Once you engage in this process, you will be astonished at the ideas and creative powers it will unleash. The following are several of the most common patterns or shorthands, and how you can subvert them.

Looking at the "what" instead of the "how":
Let us say that something goes wrong in a project of some sort. Our conventional tendency is to look for a single cause or a simple explanation, which then reveals to us how to fix the problem. If the book we are creating is not working out, we focus on the uninspired writing or the misguided concept behind it. Or if the company we work for is not performing well, we look at the products we are designing and marketing. Although we think we are being rational when we think in this way, most often problems are more complicated and holistic; we are simplifying them, based on the law that the mind always looks for shorthands.

To look at the "how" instead of the "what" means focusing on the structure—how the parts relate to the whole. With the book, it may not be working out because it is organized poorly, the faulty organization a reflection of ideas that have not been thought out. Improving the structure will improve the writing. With the company, we should look deeply at the organization itself—how well people communicate with one another, how quickly and fluidly information is passed along. If people are not communicating, if they are not on the same page, no amount of changes in the product or marketing will improve performance.

Rushing to generalities and ignoring details:

Our minds are always hurrying to generalize about things, often based on the most minimal amounts of information. We form opinions quickly, in conformity with our previous opinions, and we do not pay great attention to the details. To combat this pattern we must sometimes shift our focus from the *macro* to the *micro*—placing much greater emphasis on the details, the small picture.

In general, try approaching a problem or idea with a much more open mind. Let your study of the details guide your thinking and shape your theories. Think of everything in nature, or in the world, as a kind of hologram—the smallest part reflecting something essential about the whole. Immersing yourself in details will combat the generalizing tendencies of the brain and bring you closer to reality. Make sure, however, that you do not become lost in the details and lose sight of how they reflect the whole and fit into a larger idea. That is simply the other side of the same disease.

Confirming paradigms and ignoring anomalies:

In any field there are inevitable paradigms—accepted ways of explaining reality. This is necessary; without such paradigms we would not be able to make sense of the world. But sometimes these paradigms end up dominating our way of thinking. We routinely look for patterns in the world that confirm the paradigms we already believe in. The things that do not fit the paradigm—the anomalies—tend to be ignored or explained away. In truth, anomalies themselves contain the richest information. They often reveal to us the flaws in our paradigms and open up new ways of looking at the world. You must turn yourself into a detective, deliberately uncovering and looking at the very anomalies that people tend to disregard.

For Charles Darwin, the crux of his theory came from looking at mutations. It is the strange and random variation in nature that often sets a species off in a new evolutionary direction. Think of anomalies as the creative form of such mutations. They often represent the future, but to our eyes they seem strange. By studying them, you can illuminate this future before anyone else.

Fixating on what is present, ignoring what is absent:
In the Arthur Conan Doyle story "Silver Blaze," Sherlock Holmes solves a crime by paying attention to what did not happen—the family dog had not barked. This meant that the murderer must have been someone the dog knew. What this story illustrates is how the average person does not generally pay attention to what we shall call *negative cues,* what should have happened but did not. It is our natural tendency to fixate on positive information, to notice only what we can see and hear. It takes a

creative type such as Holmes to think more broadly and rigorously, pondering the missing information in an event, visualizing this absence as easily as we see the presence of something.

In business, the natural tendency is to look at what is already out there in the marketplace and to think of how we can make it better or cheaper. The real trick—the equivalent of seeing the negative cue—is to focus our attention on some need that is not currently being met, on what is absent. This requires more thinking and is harder to conceptualize, but the rewards can be immense if we hit upon this unfulfilled need. One interesting way to begin such a thought process is to look at new and available technology in the world and to imagine how it could be applied in a much different way, meeting a need that we sense exists but that is not overly apparent. If the need is too obvious, others will already be working on it.

E. REVERT TO PRIMAL FORMS OF INTELLIGENCE

Language is a system largely designed for social communication. It is based on conventions that everyone can agree upon. It is somewhat rigid and stable, so that it allows us to communicate with minimum friction. But when it comes to the incredible complexity and fluidity of life, it can often fail us.

In the last few hundred years, with the rapid development of the sciences, technology, and the arts, we humans have had to use our brains to solve increasingly complex problems, and those who are truly creative have developed the ability to think beyond language, to access the lower chambers of consciousness, to revert to those primal forms of intelligence that served us for millions of years.

According to the great mathematician Jacques Hadamard, most mathematicians think in terms of images, creating a visual equivalent of the theorem they are trying to work out. Michael Faraday was a powerful visual thinker. When he came up with the idea of electromagnetic lines of force, anticipating the field theories of the twentieth century, he saw them literally in his mind's eye before he wrote about them.

The reason for this "regression" to visual forms of thinking is simple. Human working memory is limited. We can only keep in mind several pieces of information at the same time. Through an image we can simultaneously imagine many things at once, at a glance. The use of images to make sense of the world is perhaps our most primitive form of intelligence, and can help us conjure up ideas that we can later verbalize. Words also are abstract; an image or model makes our idea suddenly more concrete, which satisfies our need to see and feel things with our senses.

Even if thinking in this way is not natural to you, using diagrams and models to help further the creative process can be immensely productive. Early in his research, Charles Darwin, who was normally not a visual thinker, came up with an image to help him conceptualize evolution—an irregularly branching tree. This signified that all of life started from one seed; some branches of the tree ending, others still growing and sending off new shoots. He literally drew such a tree in a notebook. This image proved extremely helpful, and he returned to it time and again.

Studies have indicated that synesthesia—moments in which the stimulation of one sense provokes another—is far more prevalent among artists and high-level thinkers. Some have speculated that synesthesia represents a high degree of interconnectivity in the brain, which also plays a role in intelligence. Creative people do not simply think in words, but use all of their senses, their entire bodies in the process. They find sense cues that stimulate their thoughts on many levels—whether it be the smell of something strong, or the tactile feel of a rubber ball. What this means is that they are more open to alternative ways of thinking, creating, and sensing the world. They allow themselves a broader range of sense experience. Stimulating your brain and senses from all directions will help unlock your natural creativity and help revive your original mind.

Step Three: The Creative Breakthrough— Tension and Insight

In the creative lives of almost all Masters, we hear of the following pattern: They begin a project with an initial intuition and an excitement about its potential success. Their project is deeply connected to something personal and primal, and seems very much alive to them.

As their initial nervous excitement inspires them in certain directions, they begin to give their concept shape, narrowing down its possibilities, and channeling their energies into ideas that grow more and more distinct. They enter a phase of heightened focus. But Masters inevitably possess another quality that complicates the work process: They are not easily satisfied by what they are doing. While able to feel excitement, they also feel doubt about the worthiness of their work. They have high internal standards. As they progress, they begin to detect flaws and difficulties in their original idea that they had not foreseen.

As the process begins to become more conscious and less intuitive, that idea once so alive in them starts to seem somewhat dead or stale. This is a difficult feeling to endure and so they work even harder, trying to force a solution. The harder they try, the more inner tension and frustration they create. The sense of staleness grows. In the beginning, their mind teemed with rich associations; now it seems condemned to a narrow track of thought that does not spark the same connections. At certain points in this process, lesser types would simply give up or settle for what they have—a mediocre and half-realized project. But Masters are stronger. They have been through this before, and on an unconscious level they understand that they must plow forward, and that the frustration, or the feeling of being blocked, has a purpose.

At a particular high point of tension, they let go for a moment. This could be as simple as stopping work and going to sleep; or it could mean deciding to take a break, or to temporarily work on something else. What almost inevitably happens in such moments is that the solution, the perfect idea for completing the work comes to them.

These stories are so common as to indicate something essential about the brain and how it reaches certain peaks of creativity. We can explain this pattern in the following way: If we remained as excited as we were in the beginning of our project, maintaining that intuitive feel that sparked it all, we would never be able to take the necessary distance to look at our work objectively and improve upon it. Losing that initial verve causes us to work and rework the idea. It forces us to not settle too early on an easy solution. The mounting frustration and tightness that comes from single-minded devotion to one problem or idea will naturally lead to a breaking point. We realize we are getting nowhere. Such moments are signals from the brain to let go, for however long a period necessary, and most creative people consciously or unconsciously accept this.

When we let go, we are not aware that below the surface of consciousness the ideas and the associations we had built up continue to bubble and incubate. With the feeling of tightness gone, the brain can momentarily return to that initial feeling of excitement and aliveness, which by now has been greatly enhanced by all of our hard work. The brain can now find the proper synthesis to the work, the one that was eluding us because we had become too tight in our approach.

The key is to be aware of this process and to encourage yourself to go as far as you can with your doubts, your reworkings, and your strained efforts, knowing the value and purpose of the frustration and creative blocks you are facing. Think of yourself as your own Zen Master. Such Masters would often beat their pupils and deliberately lead them to points of maximum doubt and inner tension, knowing such moments often precede enlightenment.

Emotional Pitfalls

When we arrive at the Creative-Active phase in our career, we are confronted by new challenges that are not simply mental or intellectual. The work is more demanding; we are on our own and the stakes are higher. Our work is now more public and highly scrutinized. We might have the most brilliant ideas and a mind capable of handling the greatest intellectual challenges, but if we are not careful, we will grow insecure, overly anxious about people's opinions, or excessively self-confident. Or we will become bored and lose a taste for the hard work that is always necessary. Better to be aware of these pitfalls in advance and never step into them. The following are among the most common pitfalls that threaten us along the way.

Complacency: In childhood, the world seemed like an enchanted place. Everything that we encountered had an intensity to it, and sparked feelings of wonder. Now, from our mature viewpoint, we see this wonderment as naïve, a quaint quality we have outgrown with our sophistication and vast experience of the real world. But our skeptical, cynical attitudes can actually cut us off from so many interesting questions, and from reality itself.

Unknown to ourselves, the mind slowly narrows and tightens as complacency creeps into the soul, and although we may have achieved public acclaim for our past work, we stifle our own creativity and never get it back. Fight this downhill tendency as much as you can by upholding the value of active wonder. Constantly remind yourself of how little you truly know, and of how mysterious the world remains.

Conservatism: If you gain any kind of attention or success for your work in this phase, you face the great danger of creeping conservatism. You begin to fall in love with the ideas and strategies that worked for you in the past. You become subtly addicted to the material comforts you have acquired and before you know it, you uphold ideas that you think you believe in, but that really are tied to your need to please the audience or your sponsors, or whomever.

Creativity is by its nature an act of boldness and rebellion. You are not accepting the status quo or conventional wisdom. You are playing with the very rules you have learned, experimenting and testing the boundaries. The world is dying for bolder ideas, for people who are not afraid to speculate and investigate.

Dependency: In the Apprenticeship Phase you relied upon mentors and those above you to supply you with the necessary standards of judgment for your field. But if you are not careful, you will carry this need for approval over into the next phase. Instead of relying on the Master for evaluation of your work, you come to rely on the opinions of the public. It is not that you must ignore these judgments, but that you must first work hard to develop internal standards and a high degree of independence. You have the capacity to see your own work with some distance; when the public reacts, you can distinguish between what is worth paying attention to and what you should ignore.

Impatience: This is perhaps the single greatest pitfall of them all. This quality continually haunts you, no matter how disciplined you might think you are. You will convince yourself that your work is essentially over and well done, when really it is your impatience speaking and coloring your judgment. Unfortunately, the creative process requires continual intensity and vigor. Each exercise or problem or project is different. Hurrying to the end or warming up old ideas will ensure a mediocre result.

The best way to neutralize our natural impatience is to cultivate a kind of pleasure in pain—like an athlete, you come to enjoy rigorous practice, pushing past your limits, and resisting the easy way out.

Grandiosity: Sometimes greater danger comes from success and praise than from criticism. If we learn to handle criticism well, it can strengthen us and help us become aware of flaws in our work. Praise generally does harm. Ever so slowly, the emphasis shifts from the joy of the creative process to the love of attention and to our ever-inflating ego. To avoid this fate, you must have some perspective. There are always greater geniuses out there than yourself. Luck certainly played a role, as did the help of your mentor and all those in the past who paved the way. What must ultimately motivate you is the work itself and the process. Public attention is actually a nuisance and a distraction.

STRATEGIES FOR REACHING THE CREATIVE-ACTIVE PHASE

As future Masters emerge from their apprenticeships, they all face the same dilemma: no one has ever really instructed them about the creative process, and there are no real books or teachers to turn to. Struggling on their own to become more active and imaginative with the knowledge they have gained, they evolve their own process—one that suits their temperament and the field they are working in. And in these creative evolutions we can detect some basic patterns and lessons for us all. The following are seven different strategic approaches to making the transition to the creative phase. They are distilled from the stories of the most creative figures, past and present.

1. The Authentic Voice

Look at a field like music. In the works of great composers or jazz artists we can detect a unique voice that comes through the music. But what is this voice? It is not something we can exactly put into words. Musicians are expressing something deep about their nature, their particular psychological makeup, even their unconscious. It comes out in their style, their unique rhythms and phrasings. But this voice does not emerge from just being oneself and letting loose. A person who would take up an instrument and try to express this quality right away would only produce noise. Jazz or any other musical form is a language, with conventions and vocabulary. And so the extreme paradox is that those who impress the most with their individuality in music are the ones who first completely submerge their character in a long apprenticeship.

By spending such time learning structure, developing technique, and absorbing every possible style and way of playing, musicians can build up a vast vocabulary. Once all of this becomes hardwired into their nervous system, their minds can focus on higher things. They can bend all of the techniques they have learned into something more personal, more authentic. And what is true for music is true for any field or discipline.

Understand: the greatest impediment to creativity is your impatience, the almost inevitable desire to hurry up the process, express something, and make a splash. What happens in such a case is that you do not master the basics; you have no real vocabulary at your disposal. What you mistake for being creative and distinctive is more likely an imitation of other people's style, or personal rantings that do not really express anything. Audiences, however, are hard to fool. They feel the lack of rigor, the imitative quality, the urge to get attention, and they turn their backs, or give the mildest praise that quickly passes. The best route is to love learning for its own sake. Anyone who would spend years absorbing the techniques and conventions of their field, trying them out, mastering them, exploring and personalizing them, would inevitably find their authentic voice and give birth to something unique and expressive.

2. The Fact of Great Yield

The animal world can be divided into two types—specialists and opportunists. Specialists, like hawks or eagles, have one dominant skill upon which they depend for their survival. When they are not hunting, they can go into a mode of complete relaxation. Opportunists, on the other hand, have no particular specialty. They depend instead on their skill to sniff out any kind of opportunity in the environment and seize upon it. They are in states of constant tension and require continual stimulation. We humans are the ultimate opportunists in the animal world, the least specialized of all living creatures. Our entire brain and nervous system is geared toward looking for any kind of opening. Our most primitive ancestors did not begin with an idea in their heads for creating a tool to help them in scavenging and killing. Instead they came upon a rock, perhaps one that was unusually sharp or elongated (an anomaly), and saw in this a possibility. In picking it up and handling it, the idea came to them to use it as a tool. This opportunistic bent of the human mind is the source and foundation of our creative powers, and it is in going with this bent of the brain that we maximize these powers.

And yet when it comes to creative endeavors, so often we find people going at them from the wrong end. This generally afflicts those who are young and inexperienced—they begin with an ambitious goal, a business, or an invention or a problem they want to solve. This seems to promise money and attention. They then search for ways to reach that goal. Such a search could go in thousands of directions, each of which could pan out in its own way, but in which they could also easily end up exhausting themselves and never find the key to reaching their overarching goal. There are too many variables that go into success. The more experienced, wiser types, are opportunists. Instead of beginning with some broad goal, they go in search of the fact of great yield—a bit of empirical evidence that is strange and does not fit the paradigm, and yet is intriguing. This bit of evidence sticks out and grabs their attention, like the elongated rock. They are not sure of their goal and they do not yet have in mind an application for the fact they have uncovered, but they are open to where it will lead them. Once they dig deeply, they discover something that challenges prevailing conventions and offers endless opportunities for knowledge and application.

In looking for facts of great yield, you must follow certain guidelines. Although you are beginning within a particular field that you understand deeply, you must not allow your mind to become tethered to this discipline. Instead you must read journals and books from all different fields. Sometimes you will find an interesting anomaly in an unrelated discipline that may have implications for your own. You must keep your mind completely open—no item is too small or unimportant to escape your attention. If an apparent anomaly calls into question your own beliefs or assumptions, so much the better. You must speculate on what it could mean, this speculation guiding your subsequent research but not determining your conclusions. If what you have discovered seems to have profound ramifications, you must pursue it with the utmost intensity. Better to look into ten such facts, with only one yielding a great discovery, than to look into twenty ideas that bring success but have trivial implications. You are the supreme hunter, ever alert, eyes scanning the landscape for the fact that will expose a once-hidden reality, with profound consequences.

3. Natural Powers

Because the creative process is an elusive subject and one for which we receive no training, in our first creative endeavors we are most often left to our own devices, to sink or swim. And in these circumstances we have to evolve something that suits our individual spirit and our profession. Often, however, we can go quite wrong in evolving a method, particularly with the pressure to produce results and the fear this instills in us. In the process many successful artists have developed for their work, we can discern an elemental pattern and principles that have wide application, built as they are on the natural inclinations and strengths of the human brain.

First, it is essential to build into the creative process an initial period that is open-ended. You give yourself time to dream and wander, to start out in a loose and unfocused manner. In this period, you allow the project to associate itself with certain powerful emotions, ones that naturally come out of you as you focus on your ideas. It is always easy to tighten up your ideas later on, and to make your project increasingly realistic and rational. But if you begin with a feeling of tightness and pressure, focusing on the funding, the competition, or people's opinions, you will stifle the associative powers of the brain and quickly turn the work into something without joy or life. Second, it is best to have wide knowledge of your field and other fields, giving your brain more possible associations and connections. Third, to keep this process alive, you must never settle into complacency, as if your initial vision represents the endpoint. You must cultivate profound dissatisfaction with your work and the need to constantly improve your ideas, along with a sense of uncertainty—you are not exactly sure where to go next, and this uncertainty drives the creative urge and keeps it fresh. Any kind of resistance or obstacle that crosses your path should be seen as yet another chance to improve your work.

Finally, you must come to embrace slowness as a virtue in itself. When it comes to creative endeavors, time is always relative. Whether your project takes months or years to complete, you will always experience a sense of impatience and a desire to get to the end. The single greatest action you can take for acquiring creative power is to reverse this natural impatience. You take pleasure in the laborious research process; you enjoy the slow cooking of the idea, the organic growth that naturally takes shape over time. You do not unnaturally draw out the process, which will create its own problems (we all need deadlines), but the longer you can allow the project to absorb your mental energies, the richer it will become. Imagine yourself years in the future looking back at the work you have done. From that future vantage point, the extra months and years you devoted to the process will not seem painful or laborious at all. It is an illusion of the present that will vanish. Time is your greatest ally.

4. The Open Field

Perhaps the greatest impediment to human creativity is the natural decay that sets in over time in any kind of medium or profession. In the sciences or in business, a certain way of thinking or acting that once had success quickly becomes a paradigm, an established procedure. As the years go by, people forget the initial reason for this paradigm and simply follow a lifeless set of techniques. In the arts, someone establishes a style that is new and vibrant, speaking to the particular spirit of the times. It has an edge because it is so different. Soon imitators pop up everywhere. It becomes a fashion, something to conform to, even if the conformity appears to be rebellious and edgy. This can drag on for ten, twenty years; it eventually becomes a cliché, pure style without any real emotion or need. Nothing in culture escapes this deadening dynamic.

We may not be aware of it, but we suffer from the dead forms and conventions that clutter our culture. This problem, however, sets up a tremendous opportunity for creative types. The process goes as follows: You begin by looking inward. You have something you want to express that is unique to yourself and related to your inclinations. You must be sure it is not something that is sparked by some trend or fashion, but that it comes from you and is real. Perhaps it is a sound you are not hearing in music, a type of story not being told, a type of book that does not fit into the usual tidy categories. Perhaps it is even a new way of doing business. Let the idea, the sound, the image take root in you. Sensing the possibility of a new language or way of doing things, you must make the conscious decision to play against the very conventions that you find dead and want to get rid of. You do not create your work out of a vacuum; your vision builds off what is missing in your field, or has turned into a cliché. You take the conventions in your field and turn them upside down. Following this strategy will give your work a kind of reverse reference point and a way to shape it.

You must not mistake newness with wild spontaneity. There is nothing that becomes repetitive and boring more quickly than free expression that is not rooted in reality and discipline. You must bring to your new idea all of the knowledge you have acquired in your field, but for the purpose of reversing it. In essence, what you are doing is creating some space in a cluttered culture, claiming for yourself an open field in which you can finally plant something new. People are dying for the new, for what expresses the spirit of the time in an original way. By creating something new you will create your own audience, and attain the ultimate position of power in culture.

5. The High End

In many fields we can see and diagnose the same mental disease, which we shall call *technical lock*. What this means is the following: in order to learn a subject or skill, particularly one that is complex, we must immerse ourselves in many details, techniques, and procedures that are standard for solving problems. If we are not careful, however, we become locked into seeing every problem in the same way, using the same techniques and strategies that became so imprinted in us. It is always simpler to follow such a route. In the process we lose sight of the bigger picture, the purpose of what we are doing, how each problem we face is different and requires a different approach. We adopt a kind of tunnel vision.

This *technical lock* afflicts people in all fields as they lose a sense of the overall purpose of their work, of the larger question at hand, of what impels them to do their work in the first place. To avoid this, your project or the problem you are solving should always be connected to something larger—a bigger question, an overarching idea, an inspiring goal. Whenever your work begins to feel stale, you must return to the larger purpose and goal that impelled you in the first place. This bigger idea governs your smaller paths of investigation, and opens up many more such paths for you to look into. By constantly reminding yourself of your purpose, you will prevent yourself from fetishizing certain techniques or from becoming overly obsessed with trivial details. In this way you will play into the natural strengths of the human brain, which wants to look for connections on higher and higher levels.

6. The Evolutionary Hijack

We generally have a misconception about the inventive and creative powers of the human mind. We imagine that creative people have an interesting idea, which they then proceed to elaborate and refine in a somewhat linear process. The truth, however, is much messier and more complex. Creativity actually resembles a process known in nature as evolutionary hijacking. In evolution, accidents and contingencies play an enormous role. For instance, feathers evolved from reptilian scales, their purpose being to keep birds warm. (Birds evolved from reptiles.) But eventually, those existing feathers became adapted for the purpose of flying, transforming into wing feathers. For our own primate ancestors living in trees, the form of the hand largely evolved out of the need to grasp branches with speed and agility. Our early hominid ancestors, walking on the ground, found this intricately developed hand quite useful for manipulating rocks, making tools, and gesturing in communication. Perhaps language itself developed as a strictly social tool and became hijacked as a means of reasoning, making human consciousness itself the product of an accident.

Human creativity generally follows a similar path, perhaps indicating a kind of organic fatality to the creation of anything. Ideas do not come to us out of nowhere. Instead, we come upon something by accident—for instance a piece of information overheard in a conversation or an ad on the radio. If we are experienced enough and the moment is ripe, this accidental encounter will spark some interesting associations and ideas in us. In looking at the particular materials we can work with, we suddenly see another way to use them. All along the way, contingencies pop up that reveal different paths we can take, and if they are promising, we follow them, not sure of where they will lead. Instead of a straight-line development from idea to fruition, the creative process is more like the crooked branching of a tree.

The lesson is simple—what constitutes true creativity is the openness and adaptability of our spirit. When we see or experience something we must be able to look at it from several angles, to see other possibilities beyond the obvious ones. We imagine that the objects around us can be used and co-opted for different purposes. We do not hold on to our original idea out of sheer stubbornness, or because our ego is tied up with its rightness. Instead, we move with what presents itself to us in the moment, exploring and exploiting different branches and contingencies. We thus manage to turn feathers into flying material. The difference then is not in some initial creative power of the brain, but in how we look at the world and the fluidity with which we can reframe what we see. Creativity and adaptability are inseparable.

7. Alchemical Creativity and the Unconscious

Our culture depends in many ways on the creation of standards and conventions that we all must adhere to. These conventions are often expressed in terms of opposites—good and evil, beautiful and ugly, painful and pleasurable, rational and irrational, intellectual and sensual. Believing in these opposites gives our world a sense of cohesion and comfort. To imagine that something can be intellectual *and* sensual, pleasurable *and* painful, real *and* unreal, good *and* bad, masculine and feminine is too chaotic and disturbing for us. Life, however, is more fluid and complex; our desires and experiences do not fit neatly into these tidy categories.

Those who think in dualities—believing that there is such a thing as "real" and such a thing as "unreal," and that they are distinct entities that can never become blended into a third, alchemical element—are creatively limited, and their work can quickly become dead and predictable. To maintain a dualistic approach to life requires that we repress many observable truths, but in our unconscious and in our dreams we often let go of the need to create categories for everything, and are able to mix seemingly disparate and contradictory ideas and feelings together with ease.

Your task as a creative thinker is to actively explore the unconscious and contradictory parts of your personality, and to examine similar contradictions and tensions in the world at large. Expressing these tensions within your work in any medium will create a powerful effect on others, making them sense unconscious truths or feelings that have been obscured or repressed. You look at society at large and the various contradictions that are rampant—for instance, the way in which a culture that espouses the ideal of free expression is charged with an oppressive code of political correctness that tamps free expression down. In science, you look for ideas that go against the existing paradigm, or that seem inexplicable because they are so contradictory. All of these contradictions contain a rich mine of information about a reality that is deeper and more complex than the one immediately perceived. By delving into the chaotic and fluid zone below the level of consciousness where opposites meet, you will be surprised at the exciting and fertile ideas that will come bubbling up to the surface.

VI

FUSE THE INTUITIVE WITH THE RATIONAL: MASTERY

All of us have access to a higher form of intelligence, one that can allow us to see more of the world, to anticipate trends, to respond with speed and accuracy to any circumstance. This intelligence is cultivated by deeply immersing ourselves in a field of study and staying true to our inclinations,

no matter how unconventional
our approach might seem to others. Through such intense immersion over many years we
come to internalize and gain
an intuitive feel for the
complicated components
of our field. When we
fuse this intuitive feel
with rational pro-
cesses, we expand
our minds to the
outer limits of
our potential
and are able to
see into the
secret core of
life itself.

THE THIRD TRANSFORMATION

For the writer Marcel Proust (1871–1922), his fate seemed set at birth. He was born incredibly small and frail; for two weeks he hovered near death, but finally pulled through. As a child, he had frequent bouts of illness that kept him at home for months at a time. When he was nine years old, he suffered his first asthma attack and nearly died. His mother, Jeanne, continuously worried about his health, doted on Marcel and accompanied him on his regular trips to the countryside to convalesce.

And it was on such trips that the pattern of his life became set. Often alone, he developed a passion for reading books. He loved to read about history, and he devoured all forms of literature. His main physical outlet was taking long walks in the country, and here certain sights seemed to captivate him. He would stop and stare for hours at apple blossoms or hawthorn flowers, or at any kind of slightly exotic plant; he found the spectacle of marching ants or spiders working on their webs particularly compelling. He would soon add books on botany and entomology to his reading list. His closest companion in these early years was his mother, and his attachment to her soon went beyond all bounds. They looked alike and shared similar interests in the arts. He could not stand to be away from her for more than a day, and in the few hours in which they were separated he would write her endless letters.

In 1886 he read a book that would forever change

the course of his life. It was an historical account of the Norman conquest of England written by Augustin Thierry. The narration of events was so vivid that Marcel felt himself transported back in time. The writer alluded to certain timeless laws of human nature that were revealed in this story, and the possibility of uncovering such laws made Marcel's head spin with excitement. Entomologists could discover the hidden principles that governed the behavior of insects. Could a writer do the same with humans and their complicated nature? Captivated by Thierry's ability to make history come to life, it came to Marcel in a flash that this would be his Life's Task—to become a writer and illuminate the laws of human nature.

At school in Paris, where he lived, Marcel impressed his classmates with his strangeness. He had read so much that his head was teeming with ideas; he would talk about history, ancient Roman literature, and the social life of bees all in the same conversation. Despite his propensity for being alone, he was incredibly sociable and a real charmer. He knew how to flatter and ingratiate himself. No one could quite figure him out or gain any sense of what the future might hold for such an oddball.

In 1888 Marcel met a thirty-seven-year-old courtesan named Laure Hayman, who was the mistress of his uncle, among many others, and for him it was instant infatuation. She was like a character out of a novel. Her clothes, her coquettish manner, her power over men fascinated him. Charming her with his witty conversation and polite manners, they quickly became close friends. In France there had long been the tradition of salons—gatherings where people of like mind discussed literary and philosophical ideas. Laure had her own infamous salon, frequented by artists, bohemians, actors, and actresses. Soon Marcel became a regular.

He found the social life in these upper echelons of French society endlessly fascinating. It was a world full of subtle signs—an invitation to a ball, or the particular seating position at a dinner table would indicate the status of an individual, whether they were on the rise or the decline. He wanted to explore this realm and learn all of its intricacies. The attention he used to direct toward history and literature he now directed toward the world of high society. He inveigled his way into other salons, and was soon mingling with upper aristocracy.

Although he was determined to become a writer, Marcel had never been able to figure out what he wanted to write about, and this had troubled him to no end. Now, however, he had his answer: this social world would be the ant colony that he would analyze as ruthlessly as an entomologist. For this purpose he began to collect characters for novels. He studied these characters, listened intently to their way of talking, followed their mannerisms, and in his notebooks he would try to bring them to life in small literary sketches. In his writing, Marcel was a master mimic.

Marcel's father, a prominent doctor, began to despair for his son. Marcel would attend parties all night, return late in the morning, and sleep through the day.

To fit in with high society, he was spending vast amounts of money. He seemed to have no discipline and no real career aspirations. With his health problems and his mother always spoiling him, his father feared Marcel would be a failure and a continuous burden. He tried to push him into a career. Marcel placated him as best he could. But in truth, he was banking everything on the publication of his first book, *Pleasures and Days*. It would be a collection of stories and sketches of the society he had infiltrated. With the success of this book, he would win over his father and all the other doubters. To ensure its success and make it into more than a book, *Pleasures and Days* would feature the beautiful drawings of a high-society lady he had befriended, and it would be printed on the finest paper.

After numerous delays, *Pleasures and Days* was finally published in 1896. The book hardly sold. Considering the printing costs it was an enormous financial fiasco, and the public image of Marcel Proust became permanently cemented—he was an elegant dandy, a snob who wrote of the only world he knew, a young man who had no practical sense, a social butterfly who dabbled in literature. It was an embarrassment and it demoralized him.

He began to grow increasingly depressed and despondent. He was tired of the salons and mingling with the rich. He had no career, no position to rely upon; as he neared thirty years of age, he was still living at home, dependent on his parents for money. He felt constantly anxious about his health, certain he was doomed to die within a few years. He heard endless stories of his friends from school becoming prominent members of society, with growing families of their own. In comparison he felt like a total failure. All that he had accomplished was a few articles in newspapers about high society and a book that had made him the laughingstock of Paris. The only thing he could rely on was the continued devotion of his mother.

In the midst of his despair he had an idea. For several years he had been devouring the works of the English art critic and thinker John Ruskin. He would teach himself English and translate Ruskin's work into French. It would consume much of his time, and he would have to put off any ideas of writing a novel. But it would show his parents that he was serious about making a living and that he had chosen a career. Clinging to this as his last hope, he poured himself into the task with all of his energy.

After several years of intense labor, a few of his translations of Ruskin were published to great acclaim. His introductions and the essays that accompanied the translations finally erased the reputation of the idle dilettante that had haunted him since *Pleasures and Days*. He was seen as a serious scholar. Through his work, he had managed to hone his own style of writing; internalizing the work of Ruskin, he could now write essays that were thoughtful and precise. He had finally gained some discipline, something to build on. But in the midst of this modest success, his network of emotional support suddenly teetered and then vanished. In 1903 his father died. Two years later his mother, unable to get over the loss, passed away as well. They had hardly ever been apart from each other, and he had dreaded the moment of her death since childhood. He felt completely alone, and he feared that he had nothing left to live for.

In the months to come he slowly withdrew from society, and as he took stock of his life up to that point he discerned a pattern that actually gave him the faintest amount of hope. To compensate for his physical weakness he had taken to reading, and in the process had discovered his Life's Task. Over the course of the last twenty years he had accumulated a vast amount of knowledge about French society—an incredibly wide variety of real-life characters of all types and classes lived inside his head. He had written thousands of pages. Using Ruskin as a mentor, in translating his works he had developed discipline and some organizing skills. He had long thought of life as an apprenticeship in which we are all slowly instructed in the ways of the world. He had served an elaborate twenty-year apprenticeship in writing and in human nature, and it had altered him deeply. Despite his ill health and his failures, he had never given up. This must mean something—perhaps a destiny of sorts. All of his failures had a purpose, he decided, if he knew how to exploit them. His time had not been wasted.

What he needed to do was to put all of this knowledge to work. This meant returning to the novel that had been trying to write for years. What it would be about, he still had no idea. The material was all there in his head. What mattered was to get to work. Something would come of it.

In the fall of 1908 he purchased dozens of notebooks, the kind he used to use in school, and began to fill them with notes. He wrote essays on aesthetics, sketches of characters, childhood memories that he strained to recall. And as he went deep into this process, he felt a change within himself. Something clicked. He did not know where it came from, but a voice emerged, his own voice, which would be that of the narrator himself. The story would revolve around a young man who becomes too neurotically attached to his mother and cannot forge his own identity. He discovers that he wants to be a writer, but he cannot figure out what he should write about. As he grows up, he starts to explore the two social realms of bohemia and landed aristocracy. He dissects the various people he meets, uncovering the essence of their characters that lies underneath their superficial social personalities. He has several failed love affairs in which he suffers the extremes of jealousy. After numerous adventures and a creeping sense of failure as he advances in life, at the very end of the novel he discovers what he wants to write—it will be the book that we have just been reading.

The novel would be called *In Search of Lost Time*, and in the end it would recount much of Proust's own life, all of the various characters he knew disguised under different names. In the course of the narration he would cover the entire history of France from the moment he was born to the present, whatever the present was. It would be a portrait of society as a whole; he would be the entomologist uncovering the laws that governed the behavior of all the inhabitants of the anthill. His only concern now was his health. The task ahead of him was immense. Would he live long enough to complete it?

Over the course of several years, he finished the first part of the book, known as *Swann's Way*. It was published in 1913, and the reviews were extremely positive. No one had ever read a novel quite like it. It seemed that Proust had created his own genre—part novel, part essay. But as he was making plans for the final half of the book, war broke out across Europe and the publishing business essentially ground to a halt. Proust continued working on the novel unremittingly, but as he did so, something strange happened—the book kept expanding in size and scope, one volume after the next. His method of working was partially responsible for this increase. He had collected over the years thousands of bits of stories, characters, lessons on life, laws of psychology that he slowly pieced together in the novel, like tiles of a mosaic. He could not foresee the end.

And as the book grew in size, it suddenly assumed a different form—real life and the novel became inextricably interwoven. He had the sensation that this social realm he was depicting had come alive within him, and feeling it from the inside, it would flow out of him with increasing ease. He had a metaphor to explain this sensation, which he included in the novel—he was like a spider sitting on its web, feeling the slightest vibration, knowing it so deeply as the world he had created and mastered.

After the war Proust's book continued to be published, one volume after another. Critics were completely astounded at the depth and breadth of his work. He had created, or rather recreated, an entire world. But this was not simply a realistic novel, for much of the work included discourses on art, psychology, the secrets of memory, and the workings of the brain itself. Proust had delved so deeply into his own psychology that he had made discoveries about memory and the unconscious that seemed uncannily accurate. Going through volume after volume, readers would have the sensation that they were actually living and experiencing this world from within, the narrator's thoughts becoming one's own thoughts—the boundaries between narrator and reader disappearing. It was a magical effect; it felt like life itself.

Straining to finish the final volume, the point at which the narrator would be finally able to write the novel we have been reading, Proust was in a hurry. He could feel his energy waning and death approaching. All through the publishing process, he would make the publishers stop the printing, as some new incident he had personally witnessed had to be included in the book. Now, sensing himself near death, he made his female attendant take some final notes. He finally understood how it felt to be dying, and he had to rewrite a previous deathbed scene—it was not psychologically real enough. He died two days later, never to see the full seven volumes in print.

KEYS TO MASTERY

Throughout history we read of Masters in every conceivable form of human endeavor describing a sensation of suddenly possessing heightened intellectual powers after years of immersion in their field. In all of these instances, these practitioners of various skills described a sensation of *seeing more*. They were suddenly able to grasp an entire situation through an image or an idea, or a combination of images and ideas. They experienced this power as *intuition*, or a *fingertip feel*.

Considering the power such intelligence can bring us, and the tremendous contributions to culture made by Masters who possess it, it would seem logical that such high-level intuition would be the subject of countless books and discussions, and that the form of thinking that goes with it would be elevated into an ideal for all of us to aim at. But oddly enough, this is not at all the case. This form of intelligence is either ignored, relegated to the inexplicable realms of the mystical and occult, or ascribed to genius and genetics.

The reason for this overall disregard is simple: we humans have come to recognize only one form of thinking and intelligence—rationality. Rational thinking is sequential by nature. We see a phenomenon A, and we deduce a cause B, and maybe anticipate a reaction C. In all cases of rational thinking, we can reconstruct the various steps that were taken to arrive at some kind of conclusion or answer. This form of thinking is extremely effective and has brought us great powers. The process that people go through when they arrive at an answer through rational analysis can generally be examined and verified, which is why we esteem it so highly. We prefer things that can be reduced to a formula and described in precise words. But the types of intuitions discussed by various Masters cannot be reduced to a formula, and the steps they took to arrive at them cannot be reconstructed. And because we recognize rationality as the only legitimate form of intelligence, these experiences of "seeing more" must either be forms of rational thinking that just happen faster, or are simply miraculous by nature.

The problem we are facing here is that high-level intuition, the ultimate sign of mastery, involves a process that is qualitatively different from rationality. And in understanding how it works, we can begin to see that such power is not miraculous, but intrinsically human and accessible to us all.

When we study something like warfare, we generally break it up into parts—field maneuvers, weaponry, logistics, strategy. Having deep knowledge of these subjects, we could analyze the results of a battle and come to some interesting conclusions. But there is an element of war that cannot be analyzed this way—the highly unpredictable aspect that comes into play when two opposing forces square up and nothing can be precisely anticipated. The situation is continuously fluid, as one side reacts to the other and the unexpected intervenes. This battle in real time has an interactive, changing element that cannot be reduced to its parts or to simple analysis, and is not something we can see and measure. We can say the same thing for an animal or anything organic.

This unseen element can be called various things. To the ancient Chinese, who understood this very well, it was known as the Tao or Way, and this Way inhabits everything in the world and is embedded in the relationships between things. The Way is visible to the expert—in cooking, carpentry, warfare, or philosophy. We shall call it the *dynamic*, the living force that inevitably operates in anything we study or do. It is how the whole thing functions, and how the relationships evolve from within. It is not the moves of the pieces on the chessboard but the entire game, involving the psychologies of the players, their strategies in real time, their past experiences influencing the present, the comfort of the chairs they are sitting in, how their energies affect each other—in a word, everything that comes into play, all at once.

Through intense absorption in a particular field over a long period of time, Masters come to understand all of the parts involved in what they are studying. They reach a point where all of this has become internalized and they are no longer seeing the parts, but gain an *intuitive feel for the whole*. They literally see or sense the dynamic.

The ability to have this intuitive grasp of the whole and feel this dynamic is simply a function of time. Since it has been shown that the brain is literally altered after approximately 10,000 hours of practice, these powers would be the result of a transformation that happens in the brain after some 20,000 hours and beyond. With this much practice and experience, all kinds of connections have been formed in the brain between different forms of knowledge. Masters thus have a sense of how everything interacts organically, and they can intuit patterns or solutions in an instant. This fluid form of thinking does not occur through a step-by-step process, but rather comes in flashes and insights as the brain makes sudden connections between disparate forms of knowledge, causing us to sense the *dynamic* in real time.

It would be a misconception, however, to imagine that Masters are simply following their intuitions and moving beyond rational thinking. First, it is through all of their hard work, the depth of their knowledge, and the development of their analytical skills that they reach this higher form of intelligence. Second, when they experience this intuition or insight, they invariably subject it to a high degree of reflection and reasoning. In science, they must spend months or years verifying their intuitions. In the arts, they must work out the ideas that come to them intuitively and rationally shape them into a form. This is hard for us to imagine, because we find intuition and rationality mutually exclusive, but in fact at this high level they operate together in a seamless fashion. The reasoning of Masters is guided by intuition; their intuition springs from intense rational focus. The two are fused.

Although time is the critical factor in attaining Mastery and this intuitive feel, the time we are talking about is not neutral or simply quantitative. An hour of

Einstein's thinking at the age of sixteen does not equal an hour spent by an average high school student working on a problem in physics. It is not a matter of studying a subject for twenty years, and then emerging as a Master. The time that leads to mastery is dependent on the intensity of our focus.

The key, then, to attaining this higher level of intelligence is to make our years of study *qualitatively* rich. We don't simply absorb information—we internalize it and make it our own by finding some way to put this knowledge to practical use. We look for connections between the various elements we are learning, hidden laws that we can perceive in the apprenticeship phase. If we experience any failures or setbacks, we do not quickly forget them because they offend our self-esteem. Instead we reflect on them deeply, trying to figure out what went wrong and discern whether there are any patterns to our mistakes. As we progress, we start to question some of the assumptions and conventions we have learned along the way. Soon, we begin to experiment and become increasingly active. At all points in the various moments leading to mastery, we attack with intensity. Every moment, every experience contains deep lessons for us. We are continuously awake, never merely going through the motions.

What made Marcel Proust's twenty years of apprenticeship qualitatively different from those of an ordinary person was the intensity of his attention. He did not simply read books—he took them apart, rigorously analyzed them, and learned valuable lessons to apply to his own life. He did not merely socialize—he strained to understand people at their core and to uncover their secret motivations. He did not merely translate, but strove to inhabit the mind of Ruskin himself. In the end, he even used the death of his mother to intensify his development. With her gone, he would have to write himself out of his depression, and find a way to re-create the feelings between them in the book he was to write. As he later described it, all of these experiences were like seeds, and once he had started his novel he was like a gardener tending and cultivating the plants that had taken root so many years before.

Like Proust, you must also maintain a sense of destiny, and feel continuously connected to it. You are unique, and there is a purpose to your uniqueness. You must see every setback, failure, or hardship as a trial along the way, as seeds that are being planted for further cultivation. No moment is wasted if you pay attention and learn the lessons contained in every experience. Never losing your connection to your Life's Task, you will unconsciously hit upon the right choices in your life. Over time, mastery will come to you.

High-level intuition is essentially driven by memory. When we take in information of any kind, we store it in mnemonic networks in the brain. The stability and durability of these networks depends on repetition, intensity of experience, and how deeply we pay attention. If we are half listening to a vocabulary lesson in a foreign language, we are not likely to retain it on any level. But if we are in the country where the language is spoken, we will hear the same words repeated in context; we will tend to pay deeper attention because we need to, and the memory trace will be that much more stable.

People who spend years studying a particular subject or field develop so many of these memory networks and pathways that their brains are constantly searching for and discovering connections between various pieces of information. When confronted with a high-level problem, the search goes in a hundred directions below conscious awareness, guided by an intuitive sense of where the answer might lie. All kinds of networks become activated, ideas and solutions suddenly rising to the surface. Those that seem particularly fruitful and appropriate stick in the memory and are acted upon. Instead of having to reason an answer through a step-by-step process, the answer comes to consciousness with a feeling of immediacy. The extremely high number of experiences and memory networks that become hardwired allow the brains of Masters to explore an area that is so wide that it has the dimensions and feel of reality itself, of the dynamic.

This high-level intuition, like any skill, requires practice and experience. At first, our intuitions might be so faint that we do not pay attention to them or trust them. All Masters talk of this phenomenon. But over time they learn to notice these rapid ideas that come to them. They learn to act on them and verify their validity. Some lead nowhere, but others lead to tremendous insights. Over time, Masters find that they can call up more and more of these high-level intuitions, which are now sparking all over the brain. Accessing this level of thinking on a more regular basis, they can fuse it even more deeply with their rational forms of thinking.

Understand: in the world today, the need to attain this high-level intelligence is more critical than ever before. To follow any career path is difficult, and requires the cultivation of much patience and discipline. We have so many elements to master that it can be intimidating. We must learn to handle the technical aspects, the social and political gamesmanship, the public reactions to our work, and the constantly changing picture in our field. When we add to this already-daunting quantity of study the vast amounts of information now available to us, and that we must keep on top of, it all seems beyond our capability.

More and more people in this overheated environment will increasingly settle on simplified ideas of reality and conventional ways of thinking; they will fall prey to seductive formulas that offer quick and easy knowledge. They will lose a taste for developing skills that require time and a resilient ego. Such people will rail against the world and blame others for their problems; they will find political justifications for opting out, when in truth they simply cannot handle the challenges of engaging with complexity. In trying to simplify their mental lives, they disconnect themselves from reality and neutralize all of the powers developed by the human brain over so many millions of years.

This desire for what is simple and easy infects all of us, often in ways we are mostly unaware of. The only solution is the following: We must learn how to quiet the anxiety we feel whenever we are confronted with anything that seems complex or chaotic. In our journey from apprenticeship to mastery we must patiently learn the various parts and skills that are required, never looking too far ahead. In moments of perceived crisis, we must develop the habit of maintaining our cool and never overreacting. If the situation is complex and others are reaching for simple black-and-white answers, or for the usual conventional responses, we must make a point of resisting such a temptation. We maintain our Negative Capability and a degree of detachment. What we are doing is gaining a tolerance and even a taste for chaotic moments, training ourselves to entertain several possibilities or solutions. We are learning to manage our anxiety, a key skill in these chaotic times.

To go along with this self-control, we must do whatever we can to cultivate a greater memory capacity—one of the most important skills in our technologically oriented environment. The problem that technology presents us is that it increases the amount of information at our disposal, but slowly degrades the power of our memory to retain it. Tasks that used to exercise the brain—remembering phone numbers, doing simple calculations, navigating and remembering streets in a city—are now performed for us, and like any muscle the brain can grow flabby from disuse. To counteract this, in our spare time we should not simply look for entertainment and distractions. We should take up hobbies—a game, a musical instrument, a foreign language—that bring pleasure but also offer us the chance to strengthen our memory capacities and the flexibility of our brain. In doing so, we can train ourselves to process large amounts of information without feeling anxious or overtaxed.

Faithfully pursuing this course over enough time, we will eventually be rewarded with intuitive powers. That whole living, breathing, changing beast that is our field will become internalized and live within us. Possessing even a part of such power will instantly separate us from all of the others who find themselves overwhelmed and straining to simplify what is inherently complex. We will be able to respond faster and more effectively than others. What seemed chaotic to us before will now seem to be simply a fluid situation with a particular dynamic that we have a feel for and can handle with relative ease.

The Return to Reality

We can identify, at certain turning points, a single ancestor from whom we humans have evolved (the first cells, simple animals, mammals, then primates). Since all life forms are descended from this common beginning, they are all interconnected in some way, and we humans are intimately implicated in this network. This is undeniable.

Let us call this interrelatedness of life the *ultimate reality*. And in relation to this reality, the human mind tends to go in one of two directions. On the one hand, the mind tends to move away from this interconnectedness and focus instead on the distinctions between things, taking objects out of their contexts and analyzing them as separate entities. At the extreme this tendency leads to highly specialized forms of knowledge.

On the other hand, there is the opposing tendency of the brain to want to make connections between everything. This generally occurs among individuals who pursue knowledge far enough that these associations come to life. Although this tendency is easier to spot in Masters, we can see in history certain movements and philosophies in which this return to reality becomes widespread in a culture, part of the zeitgeist. Perhaps the greatest example of this was the Renaissance, a cultural movement for which the ideal was the Universal Man—a person who has managed to connect all branches of knowledge and approximate the intellectual reach of the Creator.

Perhaps today we are witnessing the early signs of a return to reality, a Renaissance in modern form. In the sciences, the first seeds of this began with Faraday, Maxwell, and Einstein, who focused on the relationships between phenomena, fields of force instead of individual particles. In the larger sense, many scientists are now actively seeking to connect their various specializations to others—for instance, how neuroscience intersects so many other disciplines. We see signs of this also in the growing interest in theories of complexity applied to such disparate fields as economics, biology, and computers. We can see it in the broadening of our thinking to ecosystems, as a way to truly conceptualize the dynamic interactions in nature. We can see it in health and medicine, in the sane approach many are taking to consider the body as a whole. This trend is the future, because the purpose of consciousness itself has always been to connect us to reality.

As individuals, we can participate in this trend simply by pursuing mastery. In our apprenticeships, we naturally begin by learning the parts and making various distinctions—the right and wrong way to proceed, the individual skills to master and their particular techniques, the various rules and conventions that govern the group. In the Creative-Active we begin to melt these distinctions as we experiment with, shape, and alter these conventions to suit our purposes. And in mastery we come full circle, returning to a sense of the whole. We intuit and see the connections. We embrace the natural complexity of life, making the brain expand to the dimensions of reality instead of shrinking it to the narrowest of specializations. This is the inevitable outcome of deep immersion in a field. We can define intelligence as moving toward thinking that is more contextual, more sensitive to the relationships between things.

Think of it this way: the ultimate distinction you make is between yourself and the world. There is the inside (your subjective experience) and there is the outside. But every time you learn something, your brain is altered as new connections are formed. Your experience of something that occurs in the world physically alters your brain. The boundaries between you and the world are much more fluid than you might imagine. When you move toward mastery, your brain becomes radically altered by the years of practice and active experimentation. It is no longer the simple ecosystem of years gone by. The brain of a Master is so richly interconnected that it comes to resemble the physical world, and becomes a vibrant ecosystem in which all forms of thinking associate and connect. This growing similarity between the brain and complex life itself represents the ultimate return to reality.

STRATEGIES FOR ATTAINING MASTERY

> *The intuitive mind is a sacred gift and the rational mind is a faithful servant. We have created a society that honors the servant and has forgotten the gift.*
>
> —ALBERT EINSTEIN

Mastery is not a function of genius or talent. It is a function of time and intense focus applied to a particular field of knowledge. But there is another element, an X factor that Masters inevitably possess, that seems mystical but that is accessible to us all. Whatever field of activity we are involved in, there is generally an accepted path to the top. It is a path that others have followed, and because we are conformist creatures, most of us opt for this conventional route. But Masters have a strong inner guiding system and a high level of self-awareness. What has suited others in the past does not suit them, and they know that trying to fit into a conventional mold would only lead to a dampening of spirit, the reality they seek eluding them.

And so inevitably, these Masters, as they progress on their career paths, make a choice at a key moment in their lives: they decide to forge their own route, one that others will see as unconventional, but that suits their own spirit and rhythms and leads them closer to discovering the hidden truths of their objects of study. This key choice takes self-confidence and self-awareness—the X factor that is necessary for attaining mastery. The following are examples of this X factor in action and the strategic choices it leads to. The examples given are meant to show the importance of this quality and how we might adapt it to our own circumstances.

1. Connect to your environment—Primal Powers

The ability to connect deeply to your environment is the most primal and in many ways the most powerful form of mastery the brain can bring us. It applies equally well to the savannas of Africa as it does to any modern field or office. We gain such power by first transforming ourselves into consummate observers. We see everything in our surroundings as a potential sign to interpret. Nothing is taken at face value. There are the people with whom we work and interact—everything they do and say reveals something hidden below the surface. We can look at our interactions with the public, how they respond to our work, how people's tastes are constantly in flux. We can immerse ourselves in every aspect of our field, paying deep attention, for example, to the economic factors that play such a large role. We become like the Proustian spider, sensing the slightest vibration on our web. Over the years, as we progress on this path, we begin to merge our knowledge of these various components into an overall feel for the environment itself. Instead of exerting and overtaxing ourselves to keep up with a complex, changing environment, we know it from the inside and can sense the changes before they happen.

For our primitive ancestors, there was nothing unconventional in this approach to mastery. But for us, in our advanced technological age, such mastery involves making an unconventional choice. To become such sensitive observers, we must not succumb to all of the distractions afforded by technology; we must be a little primitive. The primary instruments that we depend on must be our eyes for observing and our brains for analyzing. The information afforded to us through various media is only one small component in our connection to the environment. It is easy to become enamored with the powers that technology affords us, and to see them as the end and not the means. When that happens, we connect to a virtual environment, and the power of our eyes and brain slowly atrophy. You must see your environment as a physical entity and your connection to it as visceral. If there is any instrument you must fall in love with and fetishize, it is the human brain—the most miraculous, awe-inspiring, information-processing tool devised in the known universe, with a complexity we can't even begin to fathom, and with dimensional powers that far outstrip any piece of technology in sophistication and usefulness.

2. Play to your strengths—Supreme Focus

There are many paths to mastery, and if you are persistent you will certainly find one that suits you. But a key component in the process is determining your mental and psychological strengths and working with them. To rise to the level of mastery requires many hours of dedicated focus and practice. You cannot get there if your work brings you no joy and you are constantly struggling to overcome your own weaknesses. You must look deep within and come to an understanding of these particular strengths and weaknesses you possess, being as realistic as possible. Knowing your strengths, you can lean on them with utmost intensity. Once you start in this direction, you will gain momentum. You will not be burdened by conventions, and you will not be slowed down by having to deal with skills that go against your inclinations and strengths. In this way, your creative and intuitive powers will be naturally awakened.

It is not simply a question of knowing deeply our Life's Task, but also of having a feel for our own ways of thinking and for perspectives that are unique to us. For instance, a deep level of empathy for animals or for certain types of people may not seem like a skill or an intellectual strength, but in truth it is. Empathy plays an enormous role in learning and knowledge. Even scientists, renowned for their objectivity, regularly engage in thinking in which they momentarily identify with their subject. Other qualities we might possess, such as a penchant for visual forms of thinking, represent other possible strengths, not weaknesses. The problem is that we humans are deep conformists. Those qualities that separate us are often ridiculed by others, or criticized by teachers. People with a high visual sense are often labeled as dyslexic, for example. Because of these judgments, we might see our strengths as disabilities and try to work around them in order to fit in. But anything that is peculiar to our makeup is precisely what we must pay the deepest attention to and lean on in our rise to mastery. Mastery is like swimming—it is too difficult to move forward when we are creating our own resistance or swimming against the current. Know your strengths and move with them.

3. Transform yourself through practice—The Fingertip Feel

In our daily, conscious activity we generally experience a separation between the mind and the body. We think about our bodies and our physical actions. Animals do not experience this division. When we start to learn any skill that has a physical component, this separation becomes even more apparent. We have to think about the various actions involved, the steps we have to follow.

We are aware of our slowness and of how our bodies respond in an awkward way. At certain points, as we improve, we have glimpses of how this process could function differently, of how it might feel to practice the skill fluidly, with the mind not getting in the way of the body. With such glimpses, we know what to aim for. If we take our practice far enough the skill becomes automatic, and we have the sensation that the mind and the body are operating as one.

If we are learning a complex skill, such as flying a jet in combat, we must master a series of simple skills, one on top of the other. Each time one skill becomes automatic, the mind is freed up to focus on the higher one. At the very end of this process, when there are no more simple skills to learn, the brain has assimilated an incredible amount of information, all of which has become internalized, part of our nervous system. The whole complex skill is now inside us and at our fingertips. We are thinking, but in a different way—with the body and mind completely fused. We are transformed. We possess a form of intelligence that allows us to approximate the instinctual power of animals, but only through a conscious, deliberate, and extended practice.

In our culture we tend to denigrate practice. We want to imagine that great feats occur naturally—that they are a sign of someone's genius or superior talent. Getting to a high level of achievement through practice seems so banal, so uninspiring. Besides, we don't want to have to think of the 10,000 to 20,000 hours that go into such mastery. These values of ours are oddly counterproductive—they cloak from us the fact that almost anyone can reach such heights through tenacious effort, something that should encourage us all. It is time to reverse this prejudice against conscious effort and to see the powers we gain through practice and discipline as eminently inspiring and even miraculous. The ability to master complicated skills by building connections in the brain is the product of millions of years of evolution, and the source of all of our material and cultural powers. When we sense the possible unity of mind and body in the early stages of practice, we are being guided toward this power. It is the natural bent of our brain to want to move in this direction, to elevate its powers through repetition. To lose our connection to this natural inclination is the height of madness, and will lead to a world in which no one has the patience to master complex skills. As individuals we must resist such a trend, and venerate the transformative powers we gain through practice.

4. Submit to the other—The Inside-out Perspective

Let us say we are trying to study and understand a very alien culture to our own. For many researchers in such circumstances, the natural response is to rely on the skills and concepts they have learned for research purposes. This would mean studying the people of this culture as closely as possible, taking extensive notes, and trying to make this alien culture fit into the framework already designated by the prevailing theories in linguistics and anthropology. Doing so, such researchers would be rewarded with articles in prestigious journals and solid positions within academia. But in the end they would remain on the outside looking in, and a good portion of their conclusions would simply be confirmations of what they had already assumed. So many elements of this culture, so different from our own, would remain unnoticed.

Part of this predilection for the outside perspective originates from a prejudice among scientists. Studying from the outside, many would say, preserves our objectivity. But what kind of objectivity is it when the researcher's perspective is tainted by so many assumptions and predigested theories? How much more can we see by moving inside and participating in this alien culture? This does not taint us with subjectivity. A scientist can participate from within and yet retain his or her reasoning powers. The intuitive and the rational, the inside perspective and science, can easily coexist.

The same applies to any group of people that we are trying to understand—the public, our audience or clients. Through continual exposure to people and by attempting to think inside them we can gain an increasing sense of their perspective, but this requires effort on our part. Our natural tendency is to project onto other people our own beliefs and value systems, in ways in which we are not even aware. When it comes to studying another culture, it is only through the use of our empathic powers and by participating in their lives that we can begin to overcome these natural projections and arrive at the reality of their experience. To do so we must overcome our great fear of the Other and the unfamiliarity of their ways. We must enter their belief and value systems, their guiding myths, their way of seeing the world. Slowly, the distorted lens through which we first viewed them starts to clear up. Going deeper into their Otherness, feeling what they feel, we can discover what makes them different and grasp their reality. This ability to understand from the inside-out is an essential part of mastery.

5. Synthesize all forms of knowledge— The Universal Man/Woman

In the Renaissance, the ideal was to become the Universal Man—a person so steeped in all forms of knowledge that his mind grows closer to the reality of nature itself and sees secrets that are invisible to most people. Today we might see this ideal of unifying knowledge as a Romantic dream, a quaint relic of the past. But in fact the opposite is the case, and for one simple reason: the design of the human brain—its inherent need to make connections and associations—gives it a will of its own. Although this evolution might take various twists and turns in history, the desire to connect will win out in the end because it is so powerfully a part of our nature and inclination. Aspects of technology now offer unprecedented means to build connections between fields and ideas. The artificial barriers between the arts and the sciences will melt away under the pressure to know and to express our common reality. Our ideas will become closer to nature, more alive and organic. In any way possible, you should strive to be a part of this universalizing process, extending your own knowledge to other branches, further and further out. The rich ideas that will come from such a quest will be their own reward.